OpenCart Theme and Module Development

Create custom themes and modules using the exciting new features of OpenCart

Rupak Nepali

[PACKT] open source *
PUBLISHING   community experience distilled

BIRMINGHAM - MUMBAI

OpenCart Theme and Module Development

First published: June 2015

Production reference: 1240615

Published by Packt Publishing Ltd.
Livery Place
35 Livery Street
Birmingham B3 2PB, UK.

ISBN 978-1-78398-768-9

www.packtpub.com

Credits

Author
Rupak Nepali

Reviewers
James Allsup
Dario Fumagalli

Commissioning Editor
Amarabha Banerjee

Acquisition Editor
Meeta Rajani

Content Development Editor
Susmita Sabat

Technical Editors
Rohith Rajan
Anushree Arun Tendulkar

Copy Editor
Vikrant Phadke

Project Coordinator
Izzat Contractor

Proofreader
Safis Editing

Indexer
Rekha Nair

Graphics
Abhinash Sahu

Production Coordinator
Aparna Bhagat

Cover Work
Aparna Bhagat

About the Author

Rupak Nepali is from Nepal. He has been working as a PHP programmer and on the OpenCart framework since 2010. He has also completed many projects and built many modules on OpenCart to meet his clients' requirements. He is currently working as a web developer at Corner Edge Interactive, Arizona, and as a freelancer on Elance, oDesk, and other freelancer sites. Rupak holds a bachelor's degree in computer information systems from Nobel College, Kathmandu, Nepal. He is currently studying for his MS degree in computer science from the Maharishi University of Management, Iowa, USA.

I have already written *Getting Started with OpenCart Module Development*. With lots of love from readers, I have been inspired to write this book. Thanks for loving my previous book, and I am sure you will love this book as well, since it covers extensions and themes.

I wish to thank my parents, especially my mother, Subdthara Nepali, and my father, Bhairab Nepali, who emphasized the importance of literacy. I also wish to thank my brothers, who helped at every step, as well as all my friends and seniors who provided me with the support and courage to write this book.

Thanks to Packt Publishing for providing me with such a great opportunity and everyone who assisted in the publishing of this book, including the reviewers.

About the Reviewers

James Allsup started developing an interest in selling online and creating websites with PHP at the age of 16. After he joined Welford Media in 2009, OpenCart became his platform of choice for e-commerce projects, shortly after his company became closely involved with its development and support. In 2012, he released OpenBay Pro, a multiple-marketplace solution that allows merchants to manage their eBay, Amazon, and Etsy stores directly from OpenCart.

Thanks to my late father. Without him, I wouldn't have been the person I am today.

Dario Fumagalli has been passionately building software since the dawn of microcomputers in 1980 and has never stopped adopting emerging technologies to increase his customers' satisfaction. From assembly code to C++, Delphi to C#, and PHP and its many frameworks to compound technologies (such as AJAX via jQuery), he has enjoyed learning every constantly changing technology and implementing it in a practical way for a result-driven business world.

In an era where the Web, mobile phones, and social networks dominate, Dario is currently implementing responsive, or adaptive, e-commerce and social media solutions. Another branch of his activities is related to securities analysis and price action trading, where he is able put into practice his software programming background to back-test strategies, implement the Monte Carlo simulation, and store financial data.

These days, he lives in Tenerife, one of the beautiful islands of the Canary Islands. He provides professional partnerships for interested companies, both where he lives and worldwide via the Internet.

www.PacktPub.com

Support files, eBooks, discount offers, and more

For support files and downloads related to your book, please visit www.PacktPub.com.

Did you know that Packt offers eBook versions of every book published, with PDF and ePub files available? You can upgrade to the eBook version at www.PacktPub.com and as a print book customer, you are entitled to a discount on the eBook copy. Get in touch with us at service@packtpub.com for more details.

At www.PacktPub.com, you can also read a collection of free technical articles, sign up for a range of free newsletters and receive exclusive discounts and offers on Packt books and eBooks.

https://www2.packtpub.com/books/subscription/packtlib

Do you need instant solutions to your IT questions? PacktLib is Packt's online digital book library. Here, you can search, access, and read Packt's entire library of books.

Why subscribe?

- Fully searchable across every book published by Packt
- Copy and paste, print, and bookmark content
- On demand and accessible via a web browser

Free access for Packt account holders

If you have an account with Packt at www.PacktPub.com, you can use this to access PacktLib today and view 9 entirely free books. Simply use your login credentials for immediate access.

Table of Contents

Preface

If you can build OpenCart themes, then you can also customize the presentation layer of OpenCart. Likewise, if you can code OpenCart's extensions or modules, then you can also customize the functionality of the OpenCart e-commerce framework and make an e-commerce site easier to administer and look better. You can also change the way the default OpenCart system works. In this book, you will learn about the third-party frameworks used in the OpenCart framework, such as Bootstrap, Font Awesome, and FlexSlider. Similarly, you will learn about the global methods used in OpenCart. We will create a custom theme and describe most of the code of the presentation layer. Then you will be able to get a description of the modules' code and create a custom module.

In OpenCart, modules are a way of customizing and extending the functionality of OpenCart. This book shows you how to create a customized theme and make all sorts of extensions: OpenCart modules, an Order Total module, the idea of creating payment and shipping modules, and ways of creating custom pages and forms on an OpenCart module to carry out insert, edit, delete, and list operations (the CRUD functionality).

This book focuses on teaching you all aspects of OpenCart's modules and themes by showing and defining code examples. We describe how to build a new theme and module from the default OpenCart theme and module. This book describes every line of code so that you will know what the code does. You will be cloning the default theme to make a new customized theme.

Each chapter teaches you how to create a new customized OpenCart theme. You will be able to create a customized theme and a Hello World module by cloning HTML. Likewise, you will get a description of every line of code of the default Featured module of OpenCart. Then we will create feedback pages used to manage feedback, and you will be able to create an Order Total module called Tips Order Total module.

Each chapter builds a practical theme and a module from the ground up using step-by-step instructions and examples.

What this book covers

Chapter 1, Getting Started with OpenCart 2.0, describes the structure of the files and folders of the default theme. This chapter shows you how to manage the layout and position of the module in a theme. You also learn the following: how to change the general settings of the images; module images; how to create and manage banners, carousels, and slideshows; and managing the layout.

Chapter 2, Bootstrap, Font Awesome, and FlexSlider in OpenCart 2 Themes, teaches you how OpenCart uses third-party frameworks, and how we can use them to design themes and modules easily, effectively, and efficiently. You get to learn these topics: why Bootstrap is used in OpenCart themes, basic templating with the use of the Bootstrap, and how to use Font Awesome and FlexSlider.

Chapter 3, Creating Custom Themes, gives a checklist to be taken into consideration for the header, footer, and other sections when creating a new custom theme. In this chapter, we change the style of the currency module, show it in a row, describe the code of the top category menu, and then style the top menu with different CSS. We describe most content area codes, such as the home, category, information, and contact us pages. We also edit CSS in a style sheet to change the background and get the knowledge to customize the theme and make a new design for the theme.

Chapter 4, Getting Started with OpenCart 2 Modules, starts off with modules in OpenCart. Here, you learn to clone the HTML content module into the Hello World module, and you are shown the way to install, configure, and uninstall an OpenCart module, and show the structures of admin and frontend files.

Chapter 5, Extensions Code, describes the code of extensions, lists all the global methods of OpenCart, shows you how to configure the feature product module, describes the code of the Featured module, shows you how to start coding for the shipping module, and describes the payment module.

Chapter 6, Create OpenCart Custom Pages, is where we create a listing page and a form page; perform actions such as data retrieval, insertion, and deletion; and show them in the frontend. You get to learn the ways to manage data and create a page to list it, insert data into the database, retrieve it (either to display or to edit), and finally delete the data. Likewise, we show you how to list the data at the frontend by creating the required page. In this way, you will be able to create modules and pages to manage data across OpenCart.

What you need for this book

You should have OpenCart installed and should have knowledge of the OpenCart backend and frontend.

Who this book is for

This book is for programmers working with OpenCart who want to develop custom OpenCart modules. You need to be familiar with the basics of OpenCart and PHP programming, and, after reading this book, you will be able to create customized OpenCart modules.

Conventions

In this book, you will find a number of text styles that distinguish between different kinds of information. Here are some examples of these styles and an explanation of their meaning.

Code words in text, database table names, folder names, filenames, file extensions, pathnames, dummy URLs, user input, and Twitter handles are shown as follows: "All CSS and JavaScript files and folders of Bootstrap are in the bootstrap folder. Likewise, all related files and folders of Font Awesome are in the font-awesome folder."

A block of code is set as follows:

```
<!DOCTYPE html>
<html xmlns="http://www.w3.org/1999/xhtml" dir="ltr"
lang="en"xml:lang="en" >
```

New terms and **important words** are shown in bold. Words that you see on the screen, for example, in menus or dialog boxes, appear in the text like this: "After editing it, you have to click on the **Image** tab."

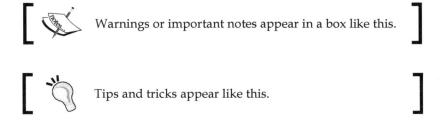

> Warnings or important notes appear in a box like this.

> Tips and tricks appear like this.

Reader feedback

Feedback from our readers is always welcome. Let us know what you think about this book—what you liked or disliked. Reader feedback is important for us as it helps us develop titles that you will really get the most out of.

To send us general feedback, simply e-mail feedback@packtpub.com, and mention the book's title in the subject of your message.

If there is a topic that you have expertise in and you are interested in either writing or contributing to a book, see our author guide at www.packtpub.com/authors.

Customer support

Now that you are the proud owner of a Packt book, we have a number of things to help you to get the most from your purchase.

Downloading the example code

You can download the example code files from your account at http://www.packtpub.com for all the Packt Publishing books you have purchased. If you purchased this book elsewhere, you can visit http://www.packtpub.com/support and register to have the files e-mailed directly to you.

Errata

Although we have taken every care to ensure the accuracy of our content, mistakes do happen. If you find a mistake in one of our books—maybe a mistake in the text or the code—we would be grateful if you could report this to us. By doing so, you can save other readers from frustration and help us improve subsequent versions of this book. If you find any errata, please report them by visiting http://www.packtpub.com/submit-errata, selecting your book, clicking on the **Errata Submission Form** link, and entering the details of your errata. Once your errata are verified, your submission will be accepted and the errata will be uploaded to our website or added to any list of existing errata under the Errata section of that title.

To view the previously submitted errata, go to https://www.packtpub.com/books/content/support and enter the name of the book in the search field. The required information will appear under the **Errata** section.

Piracy

Piracy of copyrighted material on the Internet is an ongoing problem across all media. At Packt, we take the protection of our copyright and licenses very seriously. If you come across any illegal copies of our works in any form on the Internet, please provide us with the location address or website name immediately so that we can pursue a remedy.

Please contact us at copyright@packtpub.com with a link to the suspected pirated material.

We appreciate your help in protecting our authors and our ability to bring you valuable content.

Questions

If you have a problem with any aspect of this book, you can contact us at questions@packtpub.com, and we will do our best to address the problem.

1
Getting Started with OpenCart 2.0

OpenCart is an **e-commerce** cart application built with its own in-house framework, which uses the **Model-View-Controller-Language** (**MVCL**) pattern. Thus, each theme is in the OpenCart view folder, and every module follows the MVCL pattern. In this chapter, we will describe some basic settings in OpenCart version 2.0, and help you set up the required environment for template designing, or theme designing, and module making.

The features of OpenCart

The latest version of OpenCart at the time of writing this book is 2.0.1.1, which boasts of a multitude of great features:

- Modern and fully responsive design, **OCMod** (**virtual file modification**)
- A redesigned admin area and frontend
- More payment gateways included in the standard download
- Event notification system
- Custom form fields
- An unlimited module instance system to increase functionality

Its pre-existing features include the following:

- Open source nature
- Templatable for changing the presentation section

It also supports:

- Downloadable products
- Unlimited categories, products, manufacturers
- Multilanguage
- Multicurrency
- Product reviews and ratings
- PCI-compliant
- Automatic image resizing
- Multiple tax rates related products
- Unlimited information pages
- Shipping weight calculation
- Discount coupon system

It is search engine optimized and has backup and restoration tools. It provides features such as printable invoices, sales reports, error logging, multistore features, multiple marketplace integration tools such as **OpenBay Pro**, and many more.

Now, let's start with some basic general setting that will be helpful in creating our theme and module.

Changing the OpenCart shop's general settings

Let's begin with the general settings that affect the frontend so that you will understand things you need to take into consideration when creating the OpenCart theme and module. While installing fresh OpenCart, it uses the default data and settings in the database provided by OpenCart. We describe it based on the default settings.

In OpenCart 2.0.1.1, go the address `http://localhost/packtthemeshop/admin` (if you are browsing through localhost), the admin menu will appear in the left column, and it can be extended as required by clicking on the icon in the top-left corner icons near the logo, shown here:

Now, let's start setting images' height and width.

Setting image height and width

Most of the time, developers and store administrators are confused about the image height and width, so we are covering it here. Most image sizes are managed from the admin sections, such as the category image size, product images, and so on. We can set most of the image size from the admin dashboard menu, go to **System | Settings**. Then, edit the store for which you want to edit the image size. The following screenshot shows the **Store List** from which you can select your particular store to edit by clicking on the edit icon shown in blue:

After editing, you have to click on the **Image** tab. You will notice that most of the image settings are done from here except for the module image setting. In the **Image** tab, you will see something like this:

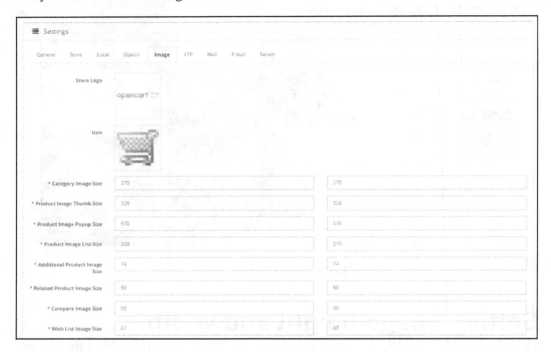

We can change the logo from here, so when designing a new OpenCart theme, we must take care to ensure that the logo is retrieved from the database. Likewise, the `favicon` icon is also inserted from the **Image** tab, so we should take care about that as well. Category image sizes are also managed from here. Let's check out the **Desktops** category page, you can see the page by hovering the cursor over **Desktops** in the menu and clicking on **See All Desktops**. This is what you will see from the default options:

Now, change the * **Category Image Size:** input field from 80 to 770, and the next field from 80 to 100 (the length is in pixels). Then, refresh the **Desktops** category page link and you will see the changes in the **Desktops** category image size. Similarly, images in the product details page are also adjustable. The product's main image is adjustable from * **Product Image Thumb Size** as well as additional product image size. The following screenshot shows the product image thumbnail and additional product images:

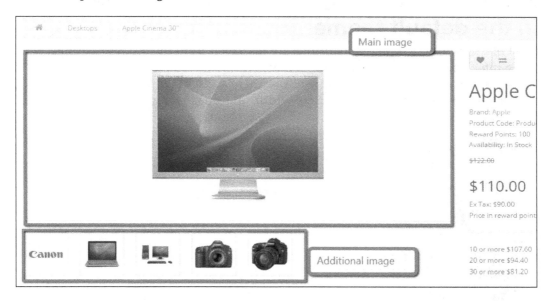

When you click on the main image or the additional image, it then pops up to show a larger image in the color box, whose image size is managed by the * **Product Image Popup Size:**.

In the same way, related products' images, the compare image size, image sizes in the wish list, and cart image sizes are all managed from image's settings page.

> **Downloading the example code**
>
> You can download the example code fies from your account at http://www.packtpub.com for all the Packt Publishing books you have purchased. If you purchased this book elsewhere, you can visit http://www.packtpub.com/support and register to have the fies e-mailed directly to you.

Managing the modules in the theme

We will now see how to manage modules in OpenCart 2.0.1.1. Layout and position play a major role in making the frontend modular. We will see how to manage modules in OpenCart 2.0.1.1.

Managing the image dimensions of modules in the default theme

Most of the module's image dimensions are managed from the module settings. So, when integrating the module into the theme, we have to take care of the settings. Consider this: in the **Latest** product module, there are settings for number of limiting the number of products to show, image width, and image height, as shown in the following screenshot:

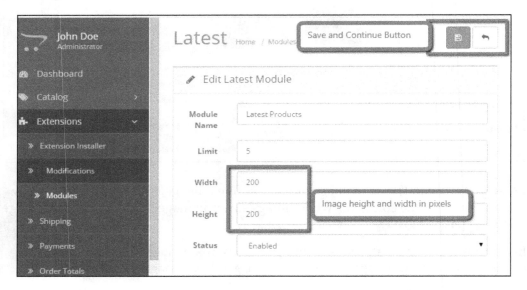

You can see this by going to the admin dashboard's menu and then to **Extension | Module**. Edit the **Latest** module. You can insert the width and height of the image to be shown in the frontend in the module. It is flexible, which means that you can show images in different sizes on different pages and positions. So, while creating the theme we have to take care of this as well.

Creating and setting a promotional banner

A **Banner** is an image shown in the top, bottom, right, or left sidebar of a website, especially for the promotions. Banners can be uploaded and customized from **Administrator** section | **System** | **Design** | **Banners**. These banners are used in the **Banner** modules, the **Carousel** module or in the **Slideshow** module. If you want to add new banners, you have to navigate to **Administrator** section | **System** | **Design** | **Banners**, then click the **Add New** button showing a + symbol and enter the banner name; after that, click on the **Add Banner** shown with a + sign button, and you will have to insert the following details:

- Banner name: Add in a suitable name for the banner
- Status: This should be set as **Enabled** to enable the banner
- Title: Enter a title that will be shown to the customer when he hovers the cursor over the banner
- Link (icon): This sets the URL to which the banner will direct the user to
- Image (icon): Upload your favorite image for the banner

The following shows the **Banners** page that has the preceding fields in it:

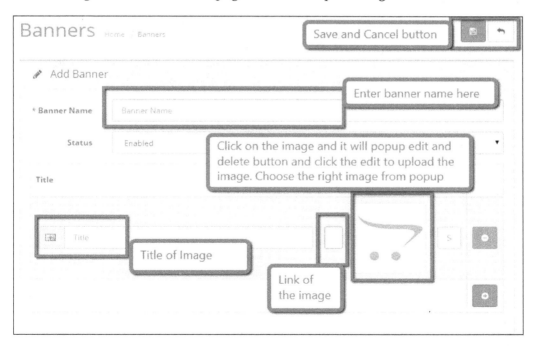

After filling in the input fields, click on the save button, and your banner is ready to use in the modules.

Installing and uninstalling a module

OpenCart is a module-based system that allows us to extend this functionality. We can add many modules and remove them as per our requirement. Go to **Administrator | Extensions | Modules**, and then click the green **+** sign to install the module. If it is already installed, you can click the red **-** sign to uninstall the module, as shown in the following screenshot:

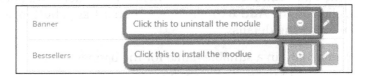

Setting the Banner, Carousel, and Slideshow modules

In OpenCart version 1.5.6.1, all layouts and positions need to be chosen while activating the module, but from OpenCart 2.0.1.1 onwards, the module section and the layout section are different. We first activate the module from the extension section, and choose the activated module and position for each layout. Let's show the **Banner** module in the home page.

Go to **Administrator | Extensions | Modules | Banner**. Then, click on the green **+** button to install; if it is already installed, click on the blue edit button. When you click on the blue edit icon, you should see the following screen:

These are the options seen in the preceding screenshot:

- **Module Name**: Enter a suitable module name
- **Banner**: This contains the settings to choose from the list of banners
- **Width** and **Height**: Insert the dimensions of the image that will be shown on the frontend; enter 180 and 150 in the **Width** and **Height** fields respectively
- **Status**: This enables the banner module

Likewise, we can activate the **Carousel** module in our OpenCart pages. Go to **Administrator | Extensions | Modules | Carousel**, and click on it if it is not installed. If it is installed, you can click the blue edit button, and then choose the banners that you wish to show, the dimensions of the images, and the status of the **Carousel** module. In a similar way, we can activate the slideshow module.

Managing the layout and position of a module in a theme

OpenCart has default page layouts that are based on the route of the page. Some of the layouts can be found by going to **Administration | System | Design | Layouts**. They are **Account, Affiliate, Category, Checkout, Contact, Default, Home, Information, Manufacturer, Product**, and **Sitemap**.

To manage layouts, perform the following steps:

1. Select any one of the layouts mentioned previously; let's consider the **Account** layout. You have to provide the layout name and then choose the **Store** and value of **Route** as **account/%**. This means that the module will be seen where the route value contains account for that store. If your URL is http://example.com/index.php?route=account/login, the module is shown as route=account. If you want to show the module in the account section where route=account, you have to add module, choose the module that you want to show, select the position in which the module lies, and insert the sort order for that module. If you don't see module in the module dropdown, then you have to install it first by going to **Administrator | Extensions | Modules**.

You can choose four positions: content top, content bottom, column right, and column left as per your wish as to where the module should be seen. The **Sort Order** field shows the module to be displayed first when there are multiple modules in the same layout and position. Then, the lower number has higher priority. Let's take an example, as shown in the following screenshot:

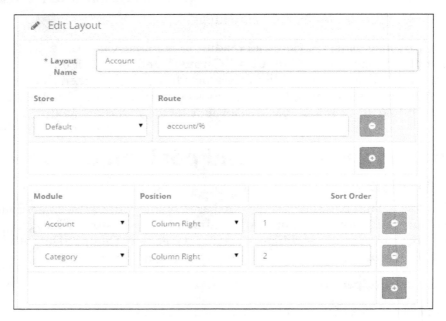

2. As seen here, we have added the **Category** module with its position set to column Right. Now, if you want to show the **Account** module at the top and the **Category** module just below it, in this case, the **Sort Order** option plays an important role. As seen in the screenshot, the **Account** module will show up first, and then the **Category** module show up below it. In this way, you can add many modules in any position and show them in any order as you please.

3. If you want to show the modules in the **Affiliate** section, you have to choose the **Affiliate** layout as the route is affiliate/%, that is, anything starting with route=affiliate/ in the URL.

4. Similarly, for other layouts, check the route at **Administrator | System | Setting | Design | Layouts | Edit**, see the route, and check the URL route; you will find where the module will show on choosing the layout name.

5. You can add a new layout from **Administrator | System | Setting | Design | Layouts** by clicking the blue plus sign at the top right corner. Then, insert the layout name, like `Special`, then click on **Add Route**, and choose the **Default** store to show in the default store, or you can choose required store and insert value of **Route** to product/special. Then, click **Add Module** and choose one of the module listed (in our case **Category**), then choose the position `Column left`, and then click on the save button to save. Now, check the front special page; you will see the category module on the left, as shown in the following screenshot:

Describing the files and folders of the default theme

Before starting to create a new theme, first you need to know the file and folder structure of the default theme. The OpenCart directory consists of mainly two interface styles: one is the **frontend**, and the other is **admin**. The frontend style is represented by the top level of the OpenCart installation folder named `catalog`, and the admin folder is `admin`. There are many other folders, such as the `system` folder, which contains classes and methods used by both the admin and the catalog.

The system folder consists of a library folder, which consists of many classes and method files such as cart, customer, affiliate, and more. The cache folder contains cache files. The database folder consists of database drivers meant for supporting different types of database engines, and the logs folder contains the error log files. Similarly, the root image folder contains all the uploaded images and the downloads folder contains all the downloadable files. The default theme files and folders are located at catalog/view/theme/default/ and are structured as shown in the following screenshot:

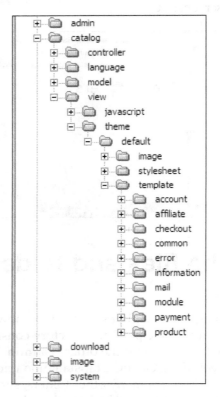

The view folder contains all the files necessary for changing the style and appearance of the presentation layer of the site. The default theme is at catalog/view/theme/default. The default/ folder contains three folders:

- image: This contains all the image files used in the theme or template file. It consists of images of buttons, reviews, menu background, payment logos, notifications (such as warning image or success image), as well as many other images that are used in the theme design.

- `stylesheet`: This folder consists of customized CSS files. In the default theme, it consists of `stylesheet.css`. The `stylesheet.css` file is the customized style sheet used in OpenCart. The `bootstrap` files are the main CSS files, located at `catalog/view/javascript/bootstrap/css`. The Font Awesome toolkit is also used, which is located at `catalog/view/javascript/font-awesome/css`. The `stylesheet.css` extends only the bootstrap CSS file and part of the theme folder. Other style sheets help in the presentation of the site, so any style sheet for the frontend are placed in the theme's `stylesheet` folder.

- `template`: The `template` folder contains multiple folders and each folder contains many template files (`.tpl`). Each folder is meant for creating a collection of related files. For example, the `product` folder contains all template files related to the products, such as `category.tpl`, `product.tpl`, `compare.tpl`, `manufacturer_info.tpl`, `manufacturer_list.tpl`, `review.tpl`, `search.tpl`, and `special.tpl`. The default `template` folder contains the following folders and each folder contains related files:

    ○ Account
    ○ Affiliate
    ○ Checkout
    ○ Common
    ○ Error
    ○ Information
    ○ Mail
    ○ Module
    ○ Payment
    ○ Product

Sometimes, we need to add our own JavaScript functionality. In that case, we can create extra folders here and insert those files. Default JavaScript files are not stored in the theme location but are in the `catalog/view/javascript` folder.

Summary

In this chapter, we described the file and folder structure of a default theme. You learned how to change the general settings of images and module images. You also learned how to create and manage banners and layouts, carousels, and slideshows. One main thing to remember is *never ever delete the default theme folder*. Always leave it in place, as it is used as a fallback if a custom theme does not have template files. So, in this way, you learned about the theme structure. In the next chapter, we will deal with basic knowledge of Bootstrap, Font Awesome, and FlexSlider of OpenCart version 2.

2
Bootstrap, Font Awesome, and FlexSlider in OpenCart 2 Themes

In this chapter, we will describe how **Bootstrap**, **Font Awesome**, and **FlexSlider** are used in OpenCart 2 themes. Bootstrap is used for responsiveness and scaffolding, Font Awesome is used to generate icons with CSS, and FlexSlider is used for a carousel and slider. These frameworks are used for rapid development of themes; introducing these frameworks helps you understand how default OpenCart themes are made and used to extend their functionality. You will learn the basics of the following topics in this chapter:

- Bootstrap
- Font Awesome
- FlexSlider

Once you excel in these frameworks, you can easily make changes to the OpenCart 2 theme and module designing part, as all default themes and the module frontend are based on these frameworks.

Bootstrap

Bootstrap is open source and is used for scaffolding to develop a responsive website using HTML, CSS and JavaScript. It is also used to manage layouts or make a presentation layer for every device. The current version of Bootstrap is 3.2.0, which has an easy learning curve.

Bootstrap is improving with age and has covered all devices. Thus, it is mobile and retina friendly, with the power of **Leaner CSS (LESS)**. LESS is one of the loved precompiled CSS languages, and is used in bootstrap to gain tremendous power and efficiency. You can visit `http://getbootstrap.com/` to get more details about bootstrap. We are just focusing on OpenCart.

Go to `http://getbootstrap.com` and click on the **Download Bootstrap** button. It will redirect to a page from where you can download the Bootstrap files.

Click on **Download source**, as shown in the following screenshot. You can download directly from GitHub as well (`https://github.com/twbs/bootstrap`); click on **Download ZIP**. Unzip the files and you will see lots of files, we will take only the required files, such as the files placed in the `dist` folder, to start the basic bootstrap template:

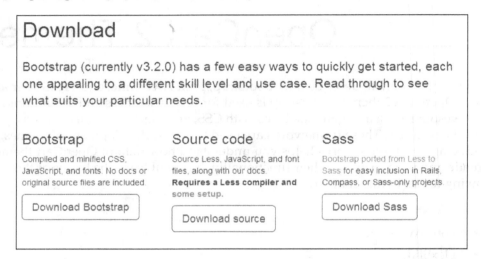

Advantages of using Bootstrap in OpenCart themes

The following can be the advantages of using Bootstrap in an OpenCart 2 theme:

- Speeds up development and saves time: There are many ready-made components, such as those available at `http://getbootstrap.com/components/`, which can be used directly in the template like we can use buttons, alert messages, many typography tables, forms, and many JavaScript functionalities. These are made responsive by default. So, there is no need to spend much time checking each device, which ultimately helps decrease development time and save time.

- Responsiveness: Bootstrap is made for devices of all shapes. So, using the conventions provided by bootstrap, it is easy to gain responsiveness in the site and design.

- Can upgrade easily: If we create our **OpenCart** theme with bootstrap, we can easily upgrade bootstrap with little effort. There is no need to invest lots of time searching for upgrades of CSS and devices.

The basic template structure with Bootstrap in OpenCart 2

The basic frontend folder structure of the presentation layer in **OpenCart 2** is like this:

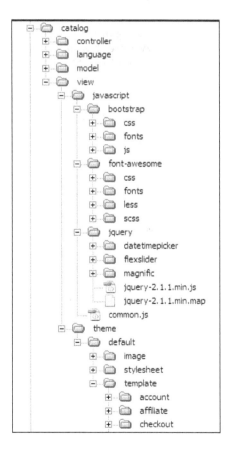

Go to the `catalog/view` folder, where you will see the `javascript` and `theme` folders. In the `javascript` folder, you will see the `bootstrap` folder, `font-awesome` folder, `jquery` folder, and `common.js` file. All CSS and JavaScript files and folders of Bootstrap are in the `bootstrap` folder.

Likewise, all related files and folders of Font Awesome are in the `font-awesome` folder. So, when designing our new theme, we should link these files and folders as per our needs. Now we'll show you some basic ideas of Bootstrap, Font Awesome, and FlexSlider so that you don't need to create your own functionality; these have covered lots of functionalities.

A basic static Bootstrap template

Let's start by creating a simple static Bootstrap template:

1. For this, let's start by downloading and then unzipping the downloaded Bootstrap. Create a folder anywhere. Name it `bootstrap`, and create the `index.html` and `stylesheet.css` in it. Next, go to the `dist` folder inside the extracted Bootstrap folder. Copy the `css`, `fonts` and `js` folders and paste them in the `bootstrap` folder which you just created. Now your folder structure will look like what is shown in the following screenshot:

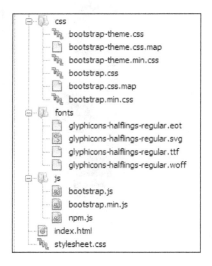

2. Bootstrap uses HTML elements and CSS properties of the HTML5 `DOCTYPE`. So, open the `index.html` file and include the following code in it:

```
<!DOCTYPE html>
<html xmlns="http://www.w3.org/1999/xhtml" dir="ltr" lang="en"
xml:lang="en" >
```

3. Specify the character set as follows:

```
<head>
<meta http-equiv="Content-Type" content="text/html;
charset=utf-8">
```

4. The following line of code instructs an IE browser to use the most updated version of its rendering engine, or to use Google Chrome Frame if it is installed:

```
<meta http-equiv="X-UA-Compatible" content="IE=edge,chrome=1">
```

5. : This code provides the rendering and zooming functionality. Add the viewport `meta` tag to the `<head>` tag. You can disable the zooming capabilities on mobile devices by adding `user-scalable=no` to the viewport `meta` tag:

```
<meta name="viewport" content="width=device-width, initial-
scale=1">
```

6. The following code defines a title for your HTML document:

```
<title>Packt Responsive Opencart Theme Tutorial</title>
```

7. The following code defines description for your HTML document:

```
<meta name="description" content="Packt Responsive Opencart Theme
Tutorial" />
```

8. The code you just saw is meant for using the Google jQuery CDN and referencing the jQuery file directly. If you use CDN, then the user may already have a cached version, which speeds up loading, reducing the bandwidth for your server that delivers the assets. But you may rely on other server or an external party to host the assets, which may be down or may be removed:

```
<script src="https://ajax.googleapis.com/ajax/libs/jquery/1.11.1/
jquery.min.js"></script>
```

9. There are many plugins, such as modals, transitions, dropdowns, scrollspy, toggle-able tabs, popovers, and many others. You can use them individually for each plugin, or use `bootstrap.js` or the minified `bootstrap.min.js` file, which includes all the plugins. It is recommended to use `bootstrap.min.js` in production because it loads faster than `bootstrap.js`:

```
<!-- Bootstrap -->
<script type="text/javascript" src="js/bootstrap.min.js"></script>
```

10. This is the extra style sheet made to override or add the extra CSS needed as per the requirement. The following code links the Bootstrap and CSS. Use only one of the `.css` Bootstrap file—either `bootstrap.css` or `bootstrap.min.css`:

```
<link rel="stylesheet" href="css/bootstrap.min.css">
<link rel="stylesheet" type="text/css" href="stylesheet.css"
media="screen" />
```

11. HTML5 elements do not work with Internet Explorer prior to version 9. So, we use **HTML5 Shiv**, which includes JavaScript and helps in better styling for unknown elements of HTML5. Thus, it is better to include HTML5 Shiv to maintain cross-browser support:

```
<!--[if lt IE 9]>
<script src="https://oss.maxcdn.com/libs/html5shiv/3.7.0/
html5shiv.js"></script>
<script src="https://oss.maxcdn.com/libs/respond.js/1.3.0/respond.
min.js"></script>
<![endif]-->
```

12. The site's content is wrapped in a container div or elements, and Bootstrap does this with its grid system. In the following code, `id="header"` is used in the custom style sheet to style the header with CSS as per our requirement. We use `class="container"` for a responsive fixed-width container, which is provided by the Bootstrap. Similarly, `.container-fluid` is used for a full-width container, which covers the entire width of your device. For best results in alignment and padding, it is better to include the rows class (`class="row"`) within `.container` for fixed width or within `.container-fluid` for full width. We can use rows to create horizontal groups of columns. In the following code, we split one of the three-column grids into two parts, one of which is the logo part of the header. Another eight-column grid is the right part of the header:

```
</head>
<body>
  <!-- Header -->
  <header id="header">
    <div class="container">
      <div class="row">
        <div class="col-md-12">
          <div class="col-md-3">This is logo part</div>
          <div class="col-md-8 pull-right">This is header right
part.</div>
```

```
        </div>
      </div>
    </div>
  </header>
  <!--/ Header -->
```

As the device or viewport size increases, the Bootstrap grid system has 12 columns. It includes predefined classes for easy layout options, as well as powerful **mixins** for generating more semantic layouts. The Bootstrap grid is seen in the following screenshot:

.col-md-1	.col-md-1	.col-md-1	.col-md-1	.col-md-1	.col-md-1	.col-md-1	.col-md-1	.col-md-1	.col-md-1	.col-md-1	.col-md-1
.col-md-8								.col-md-4			
.col-md-4				.col-md-4				.col-md-4			
.col-md-6						.col-md-6					

The following screenshot shows the grid system, its classes and the widths of devices of `http://getbootstrap.com/css/`. We used `col-md-12` in the preceding example, which means that it has a container width of 970 pixels. The other details are shown here:

	Extra small devices Phones (<768px)	Small devices Tablets (≥768px)	Medium devices Desktops (≥992px)	Large devices Desktops (≥1200px)
Grid behavior	Horizontal at all times	Collapsed to start, horizontal above breakpoints		
Container width	None (auto)	750px	970px	1170px
Class prefix	.col-xs-	.col-sm-	.col-md-	.col-lg-
# of columns	12			
Column width	Auto	~62px	~81px	~97px
Gutter width	30px (15px on each side of a column)			
Nestable	Yes			
Offsets	Yes			
Column ordering	Yes			

The `nav` tags are used for navigation and are available in Bootstrap have shared markup, starting with the `.navbar` base class, as well as shared states. We will discuss this in detail in the next chapter, when we create the menu in our OpenCart theme. For now, this is the menu section:

```html
<!-- content -->
<section id="content-wrapper" class="container">
  <nav id="mainnav" class="navbar" role="navigation">
    <div class="navbar-inner">
      <div class="container">
        This is menu part
      </div>
    </div>
  </nav>
```

In the following code, we separate into two parts the left part of the four-column grid and the content area of the eight-column grid, which is the right part of the container. Then, the section and content comment is closed:

```html
<div class="row">
  <div class="col-md-4">This is left column part</div>
  <div class="col-md-8">This is content part.</div>
</div>
</section>
<!-- #content -->
```

This is the footer part of the design that has `id="footer"`, which gives some CSS styles to the footer container and holds the full 12-column grid.

```html
<!--Footer -->
<footer id="footer" >
  <div class="container">
  <div class="row">
    <div class="col-md-12">This is footer part</div>
  </div>
  </div>
</footer>
<!--/ Footer -->
```

Like this, the `index.html` file is done. I hope you got an idea on how to play around with the bootstraps in the designing part.

Now, open `stylesheet.css` and start writing the following code to remove the margin and padding of the browser:

```
html {
  margin: 0;
  padding: 0;
}
```

The following CSS style is used to change the background color and show some of it in the body:

```
body {
  background: #f5f5f5;
  color: #fff;
  font-family:'Open Sans Condensed', sans-serif;
  line-height: 20px;
  margin: 0px;
  padding: 0px;
}
```

The following CSS code is used to provide a height of 120 pixels, a padding of 10 pixels, and a gradient background color to the header:

```
#header{
  height: 120px;
  padding: 10px;
  background-color: #23b7e5;
  background-image: -webkit-linear-gradient(left,#23b7e5 0%,#51c6ea
100%);
  background-image: -o-linear-gradient(left,#23b7e5 0%,#51c6ea 100%);
  background-image: linear-gradient(to right,#23b7e5 0%,#51c6ea 100%);
}
```

The CSS code you just saw is used to style the content-wrapper ID, which provides a minimum height of 200 pixels, a padding of 10 pixels, and a background color that is used in the content part:

```
#content-wrapper{
  padding:10px;
  min-height:200px;
  background-color: #37bc9b;
}
```

The following CSS style is used in the menu and changes the menu background color to black:

```
#mainnav{
   background-color: #2f80e7;
   margin-bottom:0px;
}
```

The following CSS style is used for the footer part, which is given a padding of 10 pixels and a background image.

```
#footer{
   padding: 10px;
   background-color: #564aa3;
}
```

Now, run index.html. You will see the output as the following screenshot:

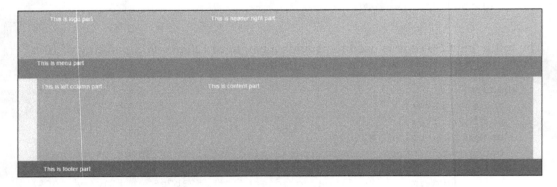

Font Awesome, an iconic font

Font Awesome CSS is an iconic font and CSS toolkit that provides scalable vector icons. It is pictographic, as it contains 519 icons that are controlled by CSS, as well as responsive. You can get more details on Font Awesome from http://fortawesome.github.io/Font-Awesome/.

We can set up Font Awesome easily by adding two lines to our website, or become a *pro* and customize it ourselves. Font Awesome supports Bootstrap 3 as well.

We get fewer JavaScript compatibility concerns with Font Awesome because it doesn't require any JavaScript. All the things are controlled by CSS, and are vectors, by which icons look awesome and gorgeous on high resolution or every device size.

Setting up Font Awesome

The easiest way to set up Font Awesome is by using the Bootstrap CDN. Or you can download the default CSS and reference the location of the CSS.

Using BootstrapCDN by MaxCDN

You can add Font Awesome using Bootstrap CDN a line of code, as shown in the following example. There's no need to download or install any file on your server:

Insert the following code into the `<head>` section of your site's HTML:

```
<link href="//maxcdn.bootstrapcdn.com/font-awesome/4.1.0/css/font-awesome.min.css" rel="stylesheet">
```

To add Font Awesome to `index.html`, open it and find this line of code:

```
<link rel="stylesheet" href="css/bootstrap.min.css">
```

Below it, paste the following lines of code:

```
<link href="//maxcdn.bootstrapcdn.com/font-awesome/4.1.0/css/font-awesome.min.css" rel="stylesheet">
```

With this, Font Awesome is ready to use.

Using default CSS

We can use the default Font Awesome CSS with the default Bootstrap CSS. For this, we have to download the CSS. So, go to `http://fortawesome.github.io/Font-Awesome/assets/font-awesome-4.3.0.zip` and download it, or go to the website and download it. Unzip the folder, find the `css` and `fonts` folders, and paste them in your `bootstrap` project's `css` and `fonts` folders.

In the `<head>` section of `index.html`, reference the location to the `font-awesome.min.css` or `font-awesome.css` file, like this:

```
<link rel="stylesheet" href="css/font-awesome.min.css"/>
```

With this, Font Awesome is ready to use. Let's check this by replacing the logo section of `index.html`. Find this code:

```
<div class="col-md-3">This is logo part</div>
```

Replace it with the following code:

```
<div class="col-md-3"><i class="fafa-shopping-cart fa-5x"></i></div>
```

You will see the shopping cart icons in the header logo. In this way, you can include many Font Awesome icons just by writing the class name and can control the icons as per the requirement.

The icons of Font Awesome

There are about 519 icons in Font Awesome 4.1.0. It contains different types of icons, such as video player, web application, medical, currency, form control, spinner, file type, text editor, directional icons, and many more

When we add Font Awesome, we can use its icons anywhere with the `<i>` tag. Some of the best examples are at `http://fontawesome.github.io/Font-Awesome/examples/`. We can use these icons anywhere using the CSS Prefix `fa` and the icon's name class. Font Awesome is designed for using inline elements, and they are mostly used with the `<i>` tag, but we can use them with `<span>` as well. A list of icons can be found at `http://fortawesome.github.io/Font-Awesome/icons/`.

For example: `<i class="fafa-car"></i>`

We can create Font Awesome icons by changing the CSS. For example, to create icons, we can increase the font size of the container where the icon is. It inherits all styles, such as drop shadow, color, and other inherited CSS.

Let's remove this code from `index.html`:

```
<div class="col-md-3">This is logo part</div>
```

In its place, paste the following code:

```
<div class="col-md-4"><i class="fafa-car fa-5x pull-left"></i><h1>Cars
Part Seller</h1></div>
```

With this change, you will see something like this:

We can increase icon sizes relative to their container. Use the `fa-lg` (33 percent increase), `fa-2x`, `fa-3x`, `fa-4x`, or `fa-5x` classes:

```
<i class="fafa-camera-retro fa-lg"></i>fa-lg
<i class="fafa-camera-retro fa-2x"></i> fa-2x
<i class="fafa-camera-retro fa-3x"></i> fa-3x
<i class="fafa-camera-retro fa-4x"></i> fa-4x
<i class="fafa-camera-retro fa-5x"></i> fa-5x
```

We have taken this screenshot from `http://fortawesome.github.io/Font-Awesome/examples/` to show how the icon size increases:

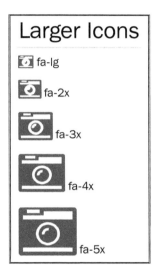

The `fa-fw` class is used to set the icons for fixed width. We can use this for `nav` lists or list groups with different icon widths and throw off alignment. Similarly, we use `fa-ul` and `fa-li` to override default bullets of lists, `fa-border` for borders, `pull-right` to float right, and `pull-left` to float left. You can see the effect in the following screenshot:

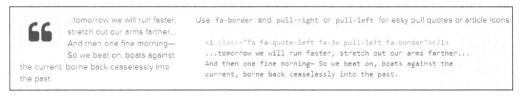

Now, let's discuss spinning icons; we can use the `fa-spin` class to rotate icons. Give the icon class name and add the `fa-spin` class. The icon keeps on spinning:

```
<i class="fa fa-spinner fa-spin"></i>
<i class="fa fa-circle-o-notch fa-spin"></i>
```

Rotated and flipped icons

If you want to flip or rotate icons, then give the icon class name and add `fa-rotate-90`, which rotates the icons by 90 degrees. Similarly, we can flip the icons by adding the `fa-flip-horizontal` or `fa-flip-vertical` class name.

The class names are shown here:

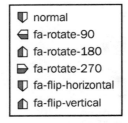

These classes can be implemented as follows:

```
<i class="fafa-shield"></i> normal<br>
<i class="fafa-shield fa-rotate-90"></i> fa-rotate-90<br>
<i class="fafa-shield fa-rotate-180"></i> fa-rotate-180<br>
```

Font Awesome supports all Bootstrap components. Also, we can customize it as per our requirements. The community of Font Awesome keeps on adding icons as per the requirement, so we can upgrade our **OpenCart** theme easily and quickly as per the trends. This is why we are using Font Awesome.

FlexSlider

FlexSlider is a free responsive jQuery slider toolkit supported by all major browsers, with many custom options and mobile support. It is simple and supports both horizontal and vertical slide orientations. It has fading animation and is supported by the latest jQuery version. Most of the code used in the upcoming steps is from the FlexSlider creator.

You can download FlexSlider from `https://github.com/woothemes/FlexSlider`. Let's get started with FlexSlider in four easy steps:

1. Link the FlexSlider CSS file and the JavaScript file.

2. We have to add jQuery, `flexslider.css`, and `jquery.flexslider.js`. You can add the following code to the head section of the code:

```
<!-- Place somewhere in the <head> of your document -->
<link rel="stylesheet" href="flexslider.css" type="text/css">
<script src="https://ajax.googleapis.com/ajax/libs/jquery/1.6.2/
jquery.min.js"></script>
<scriptsrc="jquery.flexslider.js"></script>
```

3. Now, add FlexSlider markup in the `<body>` tag of your page wherever required. Don't forget to put `class="flexslider"` and `<ul class="slides">`. This is important because FlexSlider's core CSS and JavaScript code targets this class. Your markup will then look like this:

```
<!-- Place somewhere in the <body> of your page -->
<div class="flexslider">
  <ul class="slides">
    <li><imgsrc="slide1.jpg" /></li>
    <li><imgsrc="slide2.jpg" /></li>
    <li><imgsrc="slide3.jpg" /></li>
  </ul>

</div>

</div>
```

4. Finally, add the following code to initialize and activate the FlexSlider plugin:

```
<!-- Place in the <head>, after the three links -->
<script type="text/javascript" charset="utf-8">
  $(window).load(function() {
    $('.flexslider').flexslider();
  });
</script>
```

5. Using the various options provided by FlexSlider, customize the slider as per your needs. For example, we can use the properties for advanced setups. You can see the **Advanced Options** section and learn about its different properties. We have listed some important options here. You can get more details about all of this at `http://www.woothemes.com/flexslider/`:

    ○ `namespace: "flex-"`: If we want to change the prefix, then we can use the namespace option, which is attached to the class of the element of the plug-in

    ○ `animation: "fade"` : You can change the animation type; the options available are `"fade"` and `"slide"`

    ○ `animationSpeed: 600`: You can set animation speed, which is in milliseconds

    ○ `direction: "horizontal"`: You can change the direction of sliding, which has the `"horizontal"` and `"vertical"` options

    ○ `controlNav: true`: You can create navigation that manages paging for each slide

    ○ `directionNav: true`: You can show the previous or next button

    ○ `animationLoop: true`: If this option is `true`, then images are looped; if `false`, `directionNav` will receive the disable classes at either end

    ○ `slideshowSpeed: 7000`: You can set the speed of the slideshow setting a loop in milliseconds

You can use these, and many other options, to customize your flex slider as per your requirements.

Summary

In this chapter, we saw how to use Bootstrap, Font Awesome and FlexSlider to help us design templates or themes easily, effectively, and efficiently. You now know how to use Bootstrap in OpenCart theme, basic templating with the use of the bootstrap, and how to use Font Awesome and FlexSlider. We are not sticking to only these frameworks; you can use other frameworks, such as Foundation CSS for responsiveness, bxSlider for slider, and many others as per your needs. In the next chapter, we will describe how to create a theme and enhance the functionality of the default theme.

Creating Custom Themes

3

It's time to start creating a custom OpenCart theme, since you already know the basic settings of OpenCart and its framework, including Font Awesome, Bootstrap CSS, and FlexSlider, which help us develop OpenCart themes rapidly. In this chapter, you will learn about the following topics:

- Creating custom themes by integrating HTML and CSS into a default theme
- Understanding and making changes to the code of different sections, such as headers, footers, and home pages
- Describing the code of the top menu which is the **Category** menu
- Changing the style of showing currencies, the **Category** menu, buttons, the checkout step, and the footer
- Describing the code of the home, category, product, information, and contact us pages

Preparing the files

Here are a few things to take care of before stepping into HTML and CSS to create an OpenCart theme:

1. In the `header` section, you can include a logo section, search section, currency section, language section, category menu section as well as mini-cart section. You can also include links to the home page, wish list page, account pages, shopping cart page, and checkout page. You can even show telephone numbers. These are provided by default.

2. In the `footer` section, you can include links to information pages, customer service pages (such as a contact us page), a return page, a site map page, extra links (such as brands, gift vouchers, affiliates, and specials), and links to pages such as my account page, the order history, wish list, and newsletter.

3. Include CSS modules in the style sheet, such as `.box`, `.box .box-heading`, `.box .box-content`, and so on, as clients can add many extra modules to fulfill their requirements. So, if we do not include these, then the design of the extra module may be hampered.

4. Include CSS that supports three-column structure as well as right-column-activated-two-column structure, left-column-activated-two-column structure, and one-column structure in such a way that the following happens: if the left columns are deactivated, then the right-column structure is activated. If the right columns are deactivated, then the left-column structure is activated. Finally, if both the columns are deactivated, then one column structure is activated. The following diagram shows the four styles of a theme:

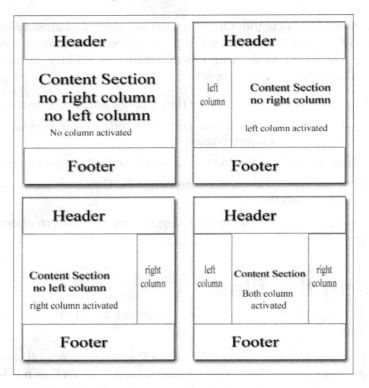

5. Include only the modified files and folders. If the CSS does not find the referenced files, then it takes them from the default folder. Try to create a folder structure like what is shown in this screenshot:

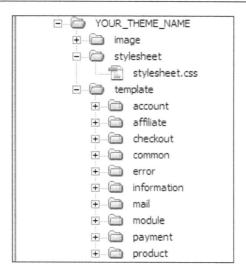

6. Prepare CSS for the buttons, checkout steps, cart pages, table, heading, and carousel.

Integrating HTML and CSS into the OpenCart theme

Once we've made our HTML and CSS ready by performing the preceding steps, we can move ahead to integrate them into our OpenCart theme. For this, we have to start by creating a new folder at `catalog/view/theme` location. We name it `packttheme`. Now we can start integrating them from the header, followed by the footer, modules and category pages, product page, and other pages.

Creating a new theme based on the default theme

So far, you've understood some general settings of an OpenCart theme. Now you are ready to create your own custom theme. As we know, OpenCart uses the MVCL pattern, so the view part is different from the core code. Therefore, we can find the OpenCart themes in the `view` folder. For the frontend, you can find the theme at the `catalog/view/theme` location, and for the admin, you can find it in `admin/view`. Right now, we are focusing on the frontend view only, so we perform our tasks in the `catalog/view/theme` folder. Let's start creating a new theme based on the default theme.

The following steps help create a new theme based on the default theme:

1. Navigate to the `catalog/view/theme` folder and create a new folder. Let's name it `packttheme`.

2. Now navigate to the `catalog/view/theme/default` folder, copy the `image` and `stylesheet` folder, go to the `catalog/view/theme/packttheme` folder, and paste it here.

3. Go to the `catalog/view/theme/packttheme` folder and create a new folder, named `template`.

4. Next, navigate to the `catalog/view/theme/default/template` folder, copy the `common` folder, go to the `catalog/view/theme/packttheme/template` folder, and paste the `common` folder there. Now the folder structure looks like this:

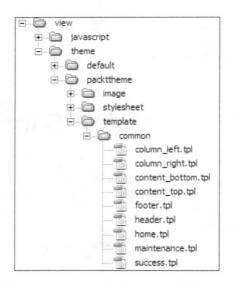

5. Open `catalog/view/theme/packttheme/header.tpl` in your favorite text editor, and find and replace the word `default` with `packttheme`.

6. After performing the replacement, save `header.tpl`, and your default base theme is ready for use.

7. Now log in to the admin section and go to **Administrator | System | Setting**. Edit the store for which you wish to change the theme, and click on the **Store** tab. Then choose `packttheme` in the template select box.

8. Next, click on save. Now refresh the frontend, and `packttheme` will be activated.

Now we can make changes to the CSS or the template files, and see the changes. Sometimes, we need theme-specific JavaScript. In such cases, we can create a `javascript` folder, or another similar folder as per the requirement.

Keep in mind that we have copied the `common` folder only; other required files are used from the default theme, so while designing the theme, we can use only the changed files. The other files are taken from the default files. The system checks whether the file exists in `packttheme` or not. If it is found in `packttheme`, it is used from there, otherwise it is used from the default folder. All of this logic is maintained in the controller, mostly near the end.

For example, you can refer to `catalog/controller/account/account.php`. You will find the following code in it:

```
if (file_exists(DIR_TEMPLATE . $this->config->get('config_template') .
'/template/account/account.tpl')) {
$this->template = $this->config->get('config_template') . '/template/
account/account.tpl';
} else {
$this->template = 'default/template/account/account.tpl';
}
```

The preceding code checks whether the file exists in the configured theme or not, and if it does not exist, then it looks for it in the default theme. Here in the code, it searches for the `account.tpl` file in `packttheme`. According to our setup, it does not find it in `packttheme`, so it searches in the default theme. If it does not find the file even in the default theme, then it produces the following error:

```
Notice: Error: Could not load template FILEPATH/catalog/view/theme/
default/template/account/account.tpl! in FILEPATH\system\engine\
controller.php on line 91
```

This means that the controller is not able to load the `account.tpl` file, so we have to create `account.tpl` in the `catalog/view/theme/default/template/account` folder.

Understanding the code in header.tpl

The `header.tpl` file is at the `catalog/view/theme/THEMENAME/template` location, and it contains all the links of CSS and JavaScript files. The same header is shown for all the pages, so we describe the code in `header.tpl`. Go to `catalog/view/theme/packttheme/template` and open the `header.tpl` file and add this to the file:

```
<!DOCTYPE html>
```

OpenCart follows the HTML5 DOCTYPE declarations, and `<!DOCTYPE html>` goes at the top of every HTML5 page. The HTML5 word `<!DOCTYPE html>` means that this page is written in HTML5:

```
<!--[if IE]><![endif]-->
<!--[if IE 8 ]><html dir="<?php echo $direction; ?>" lang="<?php echo
$lang; ?>" class="ie8"><![endif]-->
<!--[if IE 9 ]><html dir="<?php echo $direction; ?>" lang="<?php echo
$lang; ?>" class="ie9"><![endif]-->
<!--[if (gt IE 9)|!(IE)]><!-->
<html dir="<?php echo $direction; ?>" lang="<?php echo $lang; ?>">
<!--<![endif]-->
```

The `dir` attribute specifies the direction of the language to be shown. It can be LTR (left to right) or RTL (right to left). The intent of the `lang` attribute is to allow the user agents to render content more meaningfully, based on the accepted cultural practice for a given language. If you see the page source of OpenCart's pages, then you will notice something like this: `<html dir="ltr" lang="en">`. It means that the direction is from left to right and the language is English.

The following code specifies the character encoding for the HTML document.

```
<head>
<meta charset="UTF-8" />
```

The following line of code ensures proper rendering and touch zooming. It adds the viewport `meta` tag to the `<head>` tag:

```
<meta name="viewport" content="width=device-width, initial-scale=1">
```

The title for the HTML is defined as follows:

```
<title><?php echo $title; ?></title>
```

In the code you just saw `<?php echo $title; ?>` gives a title to the page as given in the language file or inserted in the backend. For example, the title of the home page is taken from the **Administrator | System | Setting** edits the store and in the **Store** tab insert `* Title:` and same will be shown in the title of the document `<title>Your Store</title>`:

The `<base>` tag specifies the base URL/target for all relative URLs in a document. If your website's URL is www.example.com, then for OpenCart, `$base` is www.example.com. So, we see `<base href="http://www.example.com/" />`:

```
<base href="<?php echo $base; ?>" />
<?php if ($description) { ?>
<meta name="description" content="<?php echo $description; ?>" />
<?php } ?>
```

The `<meta>` tag provides metadata about the HTML document. The metadata will not be displayed on the page, but will be machine parsable. The `$description` variable is given by the respective controller, and the controller either gets the data from the language or takes the content from the database. When you click on the **Desktops** category link for the default data, it shows `<meta name="description" content="Example of category description" />` when you view the source. So, it is the meta description inserted for the **Desktops** category, and the same applies to `$keywords`:

```php
<?php if ($keywords) { ?>
<meta name="keywords" content="<?php echo $keywords; ?>" />
<?php } ?>

<?php if ($icon) { ?>
<link href="<?php echo $icon; ?>" rel="icon" />
<?php } ?>
```

A **favicon (favorite icon)**, also known as a shortcut icon, website icon, tab icon, or bookmark icon, is a file containing one or more small icons. In OpenCart, the favicon is shown from the **Administrator | System | Setting** edits the store and in the **Image** tab inserts the icon, which will show something like this:

Sometimes, linking to extra links is necessary, and OpenCart uses this in its theme with the help of the preceding lines of code. When you view the source of the product details page, you will see an extra link added as canonical: `<link href="http://www.example.com/index.php?route=product/product&amp;product_id=43" rel="canonical" />`. Therefore, we need to be careful when inserting these lines of code so that the extra functionality for inserting the links from the controller is never missed:

```php
<?php foreach ($links as $link) { ?>
<link href="<?php echo $link['href']; ?>" rel="<?php echo
$link['rel']; ?>" />
<?php } ?>
```

The following code is meant for linking jQuery to the page:

```html
<script src="catalog/view/javascript/jquery/jquery-2.1.1.min.js"
type="text/javascript"></script>
```

The next code snippet links the Bootstrap CSS file and JavaScript file:

```
<link href="catalog/view/javascript/bootstrap/css/bootstrap.min.css"
rel="stylesheet" media="screen" />
<script src="catalog/view/javascript/bootstrap/js/bootstrap.min.js"
type="text/javascript"></script>
```

The following code is used to link the Font Awesome CSS:

```
<link href="catalog/view/javascript/font-awesome/css/font-awesome.min.
css" rel="stylesheet" type="text/css" />
```

Finally, this code links to the Google Fonts API's font's CSS. You can save it locally and link it to your document locally. Go to `http://fonts.googleapis.com/css?fa mily=Open+Sans:400,400i,300,700`, save the CSS file locally, and link it:

```
<link href="//fonts.googleapis.com/css?family=Open+Sans:400,40
0i,300,700" rel="stylesheet" type="text/css" />
```

Link to the style sheet, and it is now linked to the `packttheme` folder's `stylesheet.css`:

```
<link rel="stylesheet" type="text/css" href="catalog/view/theme/
packttheme/stylesheet/stylesheet.css" />
```

Sometimes, extra CSS is added as per the page, and it is never used in other pages. In such cases, OpenCart's controller calls for those required CSS files. For instance, in the product details page, when you click on the image, it pops up in the colorbox. This functionality is not used in other pages, so OpenCart's product page adds one extra style sheet file, called `colorbox.css`. The following code renders it as `<link rel="stylesheet" type="text/css" href="catalog/view/javascript/ jquery/colorbox/colorbox.css" media="screen" />`:

```
<?php foreach ($styles as $style) { ?>
<link rel="<?php echo $style['rel']; ?>" type="text/css" href="<?php
echo $style['href']; ?>" media="<?php echo $style['media']; ?>" />
<?php } ?>
```

So, we have to take this into account even when we create a new theme:

Always check whether JavaScript file is missing or not, as most of the functionalities here are controlled by `common.js`:

```
<script type="text/javascript" src="catalog/view/javascript/common.
js"></script>
<?php foreach ($scripts as $script) { ?>
<script type="text/javascript" src="<?php echo $script; ?>"></script>
<?php } ?>
```

Sometimes, an extra JavaScript file is linked as per the requirement of pages by the controllers, so this code loads the extra JavaScript files passed from the controller. For example, the extra JavaScript files `tab.js` and `jquery.colorbox-min.js` are added, and they look like this:

```
<script type="text/javascript" src="catalog/view/javascript/jquery/
tabs.js">
</script>
<script type="text/javascript" src="catalog/view/javascript/jquery/
colorbox/jquery.colorbox-min.js">
</script>
```

OpenCart 1.5.6 has the settings required to share the session cookie between stores, so the cart can be passed between different domains. The following code was a dirty hack meant to try to set a cookie for the multistore feature. In OpenCart version 2, it has been removed:

```
<?php if ($stores) { ?>
<script type="text/javascript"><!--
$(document).ready(function() {
<?php foreach ($stores as $store) { ?>
$('body').prepend('<iframe src="<?php echo $store; ?>" style="display:
none;"></iframe>');
i
});
//--></script>
<?php } ?>
```

This shows the Google Analytics code inserted at **Setting**, which is under **System** in the **Administrator** section. Edit the store. In the **Server** tab at the end, there is the **Google Analytics Code** input box. Insert the Google Analytics code in it:

```
<?php echo $google_analytics; ?>
```

The following code shows the closing `head` tag and the start of the `body` tag, which has a dynamic class name. You can see `common-home` for the home page, `product-product-PRODUCT_ID` for the product page, `product-category-CATEGORY_ID` for the category page, and `product-manufacturer-info-MANUFACTURER_ID`:

```
</head>
<body class="<?php echo $class; ?>">
```

After this, the top navigation parts started with `<nav id="top">`:

```
<nav id="top">
  <div class="container">
    <?php echo $currency; ?>
```

The preceding code shows the currencies entered and the currencies rendered from the currency module.

The following code shows the language flags if there are multiple languages entered for the store, and languages rendered from the language module:

```php
<?php echo $language; ?>
```

The multiple languages made available for the store are shown in the following screenshot:

The following code starts the right-hand menu at the top bar. It contains the $contact variable, which is linked to the contact us page, and $telephone shows the default phone number that we insert at **Administrator | System | Setting**, telephone field:

```html
<div id="top-links" class="nav pull-right">
  <ul class="list-inline">
    <li><a href="<?php echo $contact; ?>"><i class="fa fa-phone"></i></a> <span class="hidden-xs hidden-sm hidden-md"><?php echo $telephone; ?></span></li>
```

The following code shows a user icon that is linked to the account page, and a drop-down link for **My Account**, which shows the **Register** and **Login** options when the customer is not logged in. The $logged variable checks whether the customer is logged in or not. The $text_account variable shows the **My Account** text, and $account variable provides a link to the account page. You can see the use of classes such as dropdown, dropdown-menu, dropdown-menu-right, and so on. All of these are from Bootstrap CSS and are used to show the drop-down menu. Likewise, classes such as fa, fa-user, and so on are from Font Awesome CSS. If the customer is logged in, then it shows $ text_account= "My Account" linking to the account page ($account), $text_account ="Order History" linking to the order page ($order), $text_transaction ="Transactions" linking to the transaction page ($transaction), $text_download ="Downloads" linking to the download page ($download), and $text_logout="Logout" linking to the logout method ($login), which destroys the session of the customer:

```html
<li class="dropdown"><a href="<?php echo $account; ?>"
title="<?php echo $text_account; ?>" class="dropdown-toggle" data-
```

```
toggle="dropdown"><i class="fa fa-user"></i> <span class="hidden-
xs hidden-sm hidden-md"><?php echo $text_account; ?></span> <span
class="caret"></span></a>
          <ul class="dropdown-menu dropdown-menu-right">
          <?php if ($logged) { ?>
          <li><a href="<?php echo $account; ?>"><?php echo $text_
account; ?></a></li>
          <li><a href="<?php echo $order; ?>"><?php echo $text_
order; ?></a></li>
          <li><a href="<?php echo $transaction; ?>"><?php echo
$text_transaction; ?></a></li>
          <li><a href="<?php echo $download; ?>"><?php echo $text_
download; ?></a></li>
          <li><a href="<?php echo $logout; ?>"><?php echo $text_
logout; ?></a></li>
          <?php } else { ?>
          <li><a href="<?php echo $register; ?>"><?php echo $text_
register; ?></a></li>
          <li><a href="<?php echo $login; ?>"><?php echo $text_
login; ?></a></li>
          <?php } ?>
          </ul>
        </li>
```

The `$wishlist` variable gives the URL for the wish list page, and the `$text_wishlist` variable shows the **Wish List** label:

```
          <li><a href="<?php echo $wishlist; ?>" id="wishlist-total"
title="<? php echo $text_wishlist; ?>"><i class="fa fa-heart"></i>
<span class="hidden-xs hidden-sm hidden-md"><?php echo $text_wishlist;
?></span></a></li>
```

The `$shopping_cart` variable gives the URL for the shopping cart page, and the `$text_shopping_cart` variable outputs the **Shopping Cart** label on the page. The shopping cart icon is given by `<i class="fa fa-shopping-cart"></i>`:

```
          <li><a href="<?php echo $shopping_cart; ?>" title="<?php echo
$text_shopping_cart; ?>"><i class="fa fa-shopping-cart"></i> <span
class="hidden-xs hidden-sm hidden-md"><?php echo $text_shopping_cart;
?></span></a></li>
```

The `$checkout` gives the URL for the checkout page, and `$text_checkout` outputs the Checkout text and closes the top navigation:

```
          <li><a href="<?php echo $checkout; ?>" title="<?php echo
$text_checkout; ?>"><i class="fa fa-share"></i> <span class="hidden-xs
hidden-sm hidden-md"><?php echo $text_checkout; ?></span></a></li>
        </ul>
```

```
        </div>
    </div>
  </nav>
```

The `<?php if ($logo) { ?>` checks whether the logo is inserted in the **Administrator | System | Setting**. Edit the store and in the image tab input filed logo. If the logo is inserted, then it enters the `if` condition and shows the logo. The `$logo` contains the URL path for the logo, `$home` is the URL to the home page, and `$name` is the name of the store as per the header controller:

```
<header>
  <div class="container">
    <div class="row">
      <div class="col-sm-4">
        <div id="logo">
          <?php if ($logo) { ?>
          <a href="<?php echo $home; ?>"><img src="<?php echo
$logo; ?>" title="<?php echo $name; ?>" alt="<?php echo $name; ?>"
class="img-responsive" /></a>
          <?php } else { ?>
          <h1><a href="<?php echo $home; ?>"><?php echo $name; ?></
a></h1>
          <?php } ?>
        </div>
      </div>
```

The following code is meant for the search input box and search button. The `$search` variable loads the `common/search` controller, which renders `catalog/view/theme/THEMENAME/template/common/search.tpl`:

```
<div class="col-sm-5"><?php echo $search; ?> </div>
```

The output is as follows:

```
<div id="search" class="input-group">
  <input type="text" name="search" value="" placeholder="Search"
class="form-control input-lg" />
  <span class="input-group-btn">
    <button type="button" class="btn btn-default btn-lg"><i class="fa
fa-search"></i></button>
  </span>
</div>
```

In this way, the search input field and search button are shown. You can customize the search section in `catalog/view/theme/THEMENAME/template/common/search.tpl`. Don't forget to include `id="search"` and `input field name="search"`, if you like to customize the search section, as the default search is searched with JavaScript the `common.js` file using `$('#search input[name=\'search\']')`.

The following code is meant for showing the mini-cart. The `$cart` loads the `common/search` controller, which renders `catalog/view/theme/THEMENAME/template/common/cart.tpl`:

```
            <div class="col-sm-3"><?php echo $cart; ?></div>
        </div>
    </div>
</header>
```

With this, the header section is closed. We will describe the top menu categories later in this chapter.

Checklist for the header section

The checklist for the header consists of what we should not forget to include in the header while creating the new theme:

Take care of the direction and the language with `<html dir="<?php echo $direction; ?>" lang="<?php echo $lang; ?>">`. The direction and language are controlled from the language folder file. For example, for the English language, you can see the settings at `catalog/language/english/english.php`. At the top, you will see code like this, which controls the direction and the language:

```
<?php
// Locale
$_['code']              = 'en';
$_['direction']         = 'ltr';
```

When the document is rendered, you will see something like this code:

```
<html dir="ltr" lang="en">
```

Each page title is different from the others, so we should take care to ensure that the title is written as `<title><?php echo $title; ?></title>`. Then, it becomes a different title as per the page. You can see the different title on each product details. The product page takes the product name as the title. Likewise, the category page takes the category name as the title. So, we should take care of the title and it should be written as `<title><?php echo $title; ?></title>`.

Note this: never forget to enter `<base href="<?php echo $base; ?>" />` while creating the new theme, as it specifies the base URL/target for all relative URLs in a document.

After that, keep the meta-description part like this:

```php
<?php if ($description) { ?>
<meta name="description" content="<?php echo $description; ?>" />
<?php } ?>
```

This is meant for the meta-description of the document. Like the title of the page, the meta-description is also changeable as per the page, so we need to keep it as shown in the preceding code. Meta-descriptions for products and categories are inserted from the admin while inserting the product or category.

Then comes the meta-keyword part:

```php
<?php if ($keywords) { ?>
<meta name="keywords" content="<?php echo $keywords; ?>" />
<?php } ?>
```

Meta keywords are an attribute of `meta` tags, which show the keywords in the HTML of a web page and are useful for SEO in some cases. This is also different for each page, so we should write it as shown in the preceding code. Keywords for products and categories are also inserted from the admin while inserting these.

The favicon is managed from the admin, so to show at the frontend, the code should be written as follows:

```php
<?php if ($icon) { ?>
<link href="<?php echo $icon; ?>" rel="icon" />
<?php } ?>
```

In OpenCart, the favicon is inserted by navigating through the **Administrator | System | Setting** edits in the store and in the image tab insert image for the **Icon**. The same image is shown as the favicon. So, we should write the code as shown in the preceding snippet to take the favicon from the admin:

- Some links are managed from the controller, like in the product page. When you view the source of the product details page, you will see that one extra link has been added as canonical in the head section:

  ```html
  <link href="http://www.example.com/index.php?route=product/
  product&amp;product_id=43" rel="canonical" />.
  ```

- So, we need to be careful to insert these lines of code to show these extra links:

```php
<?php foreach ($links as $link) { ?>
<link href="<?php echo $link['href']; ?>" rel="<?php echo
$link['rel']; ?>" />
<?php } ?>
```

- Sometimes, extra CSS is added as per the page and is never used in other pages. In such cases, OpenCart's controller calls for those required CSS files. For instance, in the product details page, when you click on the image, it pops up in the colorbox, and this functionality is not used in the other pages. So, OpenCart's product page adds one extra style sheet file, named `colorbox.css`. We have to take this into account as well when creating the new theme, and add the following lines of code to add that extra CSS provided by the controllers:

```php
<?php foreach ($styles as $style) { ?>
<link rel="<?php echo $style['rel']; ?>" type="text/
css" href="<?php echo $style['href']; ?>" media="<?php echo
$style['media']; ?>" />
<?php } ? >
```

- When linking to extra CSS, link below it so that your extra design effects are shown.

- Never forget to link the following JavaScript files:

```html
<script src="catalog/view/javascript/jquery/jquery-2.1.1.min.js"
type="text/javascript"></script>.
```

- It points to the jQuery file. It is advised to copy your own jQuery file to your own `javascript` folder in your theme directory, and link to this new path.

- The `<script type="text/javascript" src="catalog/view/ javascript/common.js"></script>` code points to `common.js` and most functionalities are written in it, for example, adding to the cart button and the search button click functionality, and others.

- Similar to CSS, extra JavaScript is sometimes added as per the requirement of the page, and is never used in other pages. In such cases, OpenCart's controller handles JavaScript links, and the extra JavaScript is added by the following code:

```php
<?php foreach ($scripts as $script) { ?>
<script type="text/javascript" src="<?php echo $script; ?>">
</script>
<?php } ?>
```

- You can insert the Google Analytics code at **Administrator | System | Settings**. Edit the store, and in the **Server** tab at the end, there is the **Google Analytics Code** input box. The same Google Analytics code is shown in the front in the header using this line:

```
<?php echo $google_analytics; ?>
```

So, you should not forget to insert this code to work with Google Analytics.

These nine points constitute the checklist that you should remember to insert in the header part while creating a new OpenCart theme. You can add extra JavaScript and style sheets as per your requirement to create a new theme.

Changing the style of currency

The currency, language, search, and a mini-shopping cart in the header are invoked as modules in the header. We are going to change the style used to show the currency. The default style of the currency is shown in a dropdown, and we are changing it to show up in a row, like this:

Go to `catalog/view/theme/packttheme/template/common` and open `currency.tpl`. Always remember to create a copy in the new theme folder to make the changes; never make the changes in the default folder. We should not make changes in the default folder because while updating the version of the OpenCart, it will be overridden by the default files, and all the changes made will be removed.

Now open `catalog/view/theme/packttheme/template/module/currency.tpl` in your favourite text editor, remove all of the existing code, and type the following code. We will describe each line afterwards:

```php
<?php if (count($currencies) > 1) { ?>
<form action="<?php echo $action; ?>" method="post"
enctype="multipart/form-data" id="currency">
  <?php foreach ($currencies as $currency) { ?>
  <div class="pull-left">
    <?php if ($currency['symbol_left']) { ?>
```

```
      <button class="currency-select btn btn-link btn-block"
type="button" name="<?php echo $currency['code']; ?>"><?php echo
$currency['symbol_left']; ?> </button>
      <?php } else { ?>
      <button class="currency-select btn btn-link btn-block"
type="button" name="<?php echo $currency['code']; ?>"><?php echo
$currency['symbol_right']; ?> </button>
      <?php } ?>
  </div>
  <?php } ?>
  <input type="hidden" name="code" value="" />
  <input type="hidden" name="redirect" value="<?php echo $redirect;
?>" />
</form>
<?php } ?>
```

Now save the file and refresh the frontend. You will see the changed currency as the effect of the preceding code.

In the preceding code, `<?php if(count($currencies) > 1) { ?>` checks whether there is more than one currency or not. The currencies are shown only if there are two or more of them.

The following code is used to start the form:

```
<form action="<?php echo $action; ?>" method="post"
enctype="multipart/form-data">
```

After rendering, it looks like this:

```
<form action="http://www.example.com/index.php?route=common/currency/
currency" method="post" enctype="multipart/form-data"  id="currency">
```

When you select another currency, it is submitted to `route= common/currency/currency`. The ID currency div is used in CSS to manage the style and position:

```
  <?php foreach ($currencies as $currency) { ?>
```

This code is the iteration of the currencies array:

```
<?php if ($currency['symbol_left']) { ?>
    <button class="currency-select btn btn-link btn-block"
type="button" name="<?php echo $currency['code']; ?>"><?php echo
$currency['symbol_left']; ?> </button>
    <?php } else { ?>
    <button class="currency-select btn btn-link btn-block"
type="button" name="<?php echo $currency['code']; ?>"><?php echo
$currency['symbol_right']; ?> </button>
    <?php } ?>
```

For some currencies, the symbol is to the right of the price, and for some, it is to the left of the price. So, OpenCart has made room for the occurrence of symbols for both sides. The `$currency['symbol_left']` and `$currency['symbol_right']` show the currency, and `$currency['code']` holds the currency name:

```
<input type="hidden" name="code" value="" />
```

The value of the input box named `code` becomes the currency code when the selection is made, and the form is submitted with the chosen value. With this currency code value, the currency is set all over the site:

```
<input type="hidden" name="redirect" value="<?php echo $redirect; ?>"
/>
</form>
<?php } ?>
```

The value of the input box named `redirect` becomes the current active URL when the currency is changed the redirect value is submitted. After the currency is set, it is redirected to the current URL. The closing tag of the form and the closing braces are meant to check whether there is more than one currency. In this way, you can change the style of the language as well.

Describing the code of the top menu categories

We'll describe the categories that show the menu's code, and then we will change the style of the menu. Go to `catalog/view/theme/packttheme/template/common/`, open `header.tpl` in your favourite editor, and find `<?php if ($categories) { ?>`. We are going to describe the code that shows up in the category menu:

```
<?php if ($categories) { ?>
<div class="container">
  <nav id="menu" class="navbar">
```

The preceding code checks whether there is a category or not:

```
<div class="navbar-header"><span id="category" class="visible-
xs"><?php echo $text_category; ?></span>
    <button type="button" class="btn btn-navbar navbar-toggle" data-
toggle="collapse" data-target=".navbar-ex1-collapse"><i class="fa fa-
bars"></i></button>
    </div>
```

This div is shown only for extra-small devices, as it uses the visible-xs class, collapses the menu, and shows the text category, as shown in the following screenshot:

The following code is used to iterate through top showing categories and check whether the category has children:

```
<div class="collapse navbar-collapse navbar-ex1-collapse">
  <ul class="nav navbar-nav">
    <?php foreach ($categories as $category) { ?>
    <?php if ($category['children']) { ?>
```

The following code shows the top-level category name and the dropdown of the child categories:

```
<li class="dropdown"><a href="<?php echo $category['href'];
?>" class="dropdown-toggle" data-toggle="dropdown"><?php echo
$category['name']; ?></a>
```

The next code snippet will show you the child categories:

```
<div class="dropdown-menu">
  <div class="dropdown-inner">
    <?php foreach (array_chunk($category['children'], ceil(c
ount($category['children']) / $category['column'])) as $children) { ?>
    <ul class="list-unstyled">
      <?php foreach ($children as $child) { ?>
      <li><a href="<?php echo $child['href']; ?>"><?php echo
$child['name']; ?></a></li>
      <?php } ?>
    </ul>
    <?php } ?>
  </div>
```

The following code is used to show the **See All** top category name and the link to the category page:

```
<a href="<?php echo $category['href']; ?>" class="see-
all"><?php echo $text_all; ?> <?php echo $category['name']; ?></a>
```

The code you just saw is used to show the top category name and link to it if it does not have a child category:

```
</div>
      </li>
      <?php } else { ?>
      <li><a href="<?php echo $category['href']; ?>"><?php echo
$category['name']; ?></a></li>
```

The following code is used to show the top-level categories and their subcategories:

```
      <?php } ?>
      <?php } ?>
    </ul>
  </div>
</nav>
</div>
<?php } ?>
```

The $categories variable includes top-level categories only when we tick the **Top** checkbox while inserting the category and its subcategories:

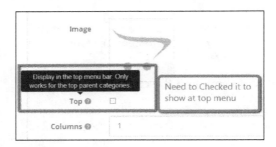

$category['name'] is meant for the top-level category name and
$category['href'] for its link. $category['children'] contains the subcategories.
$category['column'] is the number of columns to be used for the bottom three categories, and it works only for the top parent categories. The <a href="<?php echo $category['href']; ?>" class="see-all"><?php echo $text_all; ?> <?php echo $category['name']; ?></a> code shows **See All CATEGORY_NAME**, which links it to the top category.

Changing the style of the menu

We are going to change the style of the default menu bar's background to make it orange. For this, we simply make an adjustment to the style sheet. Go to `catalog/view/theme/packttheme/stylesheet/` and open `stylesheet.css` in your favorite editor. Go to the end of the style sheet and paste the following CSS code:

```css
#menu {
    background-color: #e84e1b;
    background-image: linear-gradient(to bottom, #e84e1b, #c93a17);
    background-repeat: repeat-x;
    border-color: #e84e1b #e84e1b #e84e1b;
    min-height: 40px;
}
```

Understanding the code in footer.tpl

The `footer.tpl` is located at `catalog/view/theme/THEMENAME/template/common/footer.tpl`, and it contains all the links to information pages and extra links to other pages. The same footer is shown for all the pages, so we describe the code in `footer.tpl`:

```php
<footer>
  <div class="container">
    <div class="row">
<?php if ($informations) { ?>
      <div class="col-sm-3">
        <h5><?php echo $text_information; ?></h5>
        <ul class="list-unstyled">
          <?php foreach ($informations as $information) { ?>
          <li><a href="<?php echo $information['href']; ?>"><?php echo $information['title']; ?></a></li>
          <?php } ?>
        </ul>
      </div>
      <?php } ?>
```

The preceding code starts the div with ID as the footer. It checks whether there are any information pages or not. The information pages are inserted from information that can be found by going to **Administrator | Catalog**. The $text_information shows the **Information** text from the catalog/language/english/common/ footer.php language file. If there are information pages, then it loops to show the information page title linked to those pages. $information['href'] is the link, and $information['title'] is the title:

```
<div class="col-sm-3">
    <h5><?php echo $text_service; ?></h5>
    <ul class="list-unstyled">
        <li><a href="<?php echo $contact; ?>"><?php echo $text_
contact; ?></a></li>
        <li><a href="<?php echo $return; ?>"><?php echo $text_
return; ?></a></li>
        <li><a href="<?php echo $sitemap; ?>"><?php echo $text_
sitemap; ?></a></li>
    </ul>
</div>
```

All texts are shown from the language file and linked to the pages in the preceding code. For example, $text_contact shows the **Contact** text and is linked to the contact us page, and similarly to all other pages:

```
<div class="col-sm-3">
    <h5><?php echo $text_extra; ?></h5>
    <ul class="list-unstyled">
        <li><a href="<?php echo $manufacturer; ?>"><?php echo $text_
manufacturer; ?></a></li>
        <li><a href="<?php echo $voucher; ?>"><?php echo $text_
voucher; ?></a></li>
        <li><a href="<?php echo $affiliate; ?>"><?php echo $text_
affiliate; ?></a></li>
        <li><a href="<?php echo $special; ?>"><?php echo $text_
special; ?></a></li>
    </ul>
</div>
```

Texts shown in the footer from the language file and is linked to pages in the preceding code. For example, $text_manufacturer shows the **Manufacturer** text and is linked to the manufacturer page, and the same is true for other pages.

```
<div class="col-sm-3">
    <h5><?php echo $text_account; ?></h5>
    <ul class="list-unstyled">
```

```
        <li><a href="<?php echo $account; ?>"><?php echo $text_
account; ?></a></li>
        <li><a href="<?php echo $order; ?>"><?php echo $text_order;
?></a></li>
        <li><a href="<?php echo $wishlist; ?>"><?php echo $text_
wishlist; ?></a></li>
        <li><a href="<?php echo $newsletter; ?>"><?php echo $text_
newsletter; ?></a></li>
      </ul>
    </div>
  </div>
  <hr>
  <p><?php echo $powered; ?></p>
  </div>
</footer>
```

The code you just saw is used to show the links to the account pages in the footer. $text_account shows **Account** and is linked to the account page:

```
<!--
OpenCart is open source software and you are free to remove the
powered by OpenCart if you want, but its generally accepted practise
to make a small donation.
Please donate via PayPal to donate@opencart.com
//-->
<!-- Theme created by Welford Media for OpenCart 2.0 www.welfordmedia.
co.uk -->
</body></html>
```

These lines of code show the comments describing the Opencart and the PayPal e-mail that we can donate to PayPal, and the closing tags of the div container, body, and html.

In a popular customized theme, you can see extra JavaScripts loaded in the footer section, which will load the content first and then the JavaScripts, making it look like it loads faster.

Changing the style of the footer div in the footer

We are going to change the wrapping box of the footer to make it look like this:

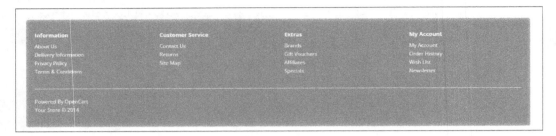

We just have to change the CSS in `sytlesheet.css` at `catalog/view/theme/packttheme/stylesheet/stylesheet.css`. Open `stylesheet.css` and add the following CSS to see the changes:

```
footer {
  margin-top: 0px;
  padding-top: 0px;
  background-color: #fff;
  border-top:none;
  color: #fff;
}
footer a {
  color:#fff;
}
footer hr {
  border-bottom: 1px solid #fff;
}
footer .container {
  background-color: #e84e1b;
  min-height: 40px;
  margin-bottom: 10px;
  padding: 20px 20px 20px 20px;
  overflow: hidden;
  border: 1px solid #fff;
  box-shadow: inset 0px 0px 45px pink;
  -webkit-box-shadow: inset 0px 0px 15px pink;
  -moz-box-shadow: inset 0px 0px 15px pink;
  border-radius: 5px 5px 5px 5px;
```

```
-webkit-border-radius: 5px 5px 5px 5px;
-moz-border-radius: 5px 5px 5px 5px;
clear: both;

}
```

The `<footer>` tag defines a footer for a document or section. We override the `<footer>` CSS to show the orange background, remove the top border, and change the text color to white. We use the `box-shadow` CSS property for the footer container, though it is not widely supported by browsers. For Firefox support, we used `-moz-box-shadow`, and for Safari/WebKit, we used `-webkit-box-shadow`. Similarly for the `border-radius`, for Firefox, we used `-moz-border-radius`. For Safari/WebKit we used `-webkit-border-radius`. In this way, we changed the style of the footer.

Removing the copyright information in the footer

Although we did not recommend removing the copyright from the footer, most of us need to do it, so we'll show you how to remove the copyright from the footer. Go to `catalog/view/theme/packttheme/template/common/`, open `footer.tpl`, and find the following lines of code:

```
<p><?php echo $powered; ?></p>
```

Remove this code and the copyright will removed. Now, you can place your own copyright sentences.

Although not recommended, another way is to go to `catalog/language/english/common/footer.php` and find the following line:

```
$_['text_powered']       = 'Powered By <a href="http://www.opencart.
com">OpenCart</a><br /> %s &copy; %s';
```

Change this text as per your requirements. You need to know that the first `%s` sign shows your store name and the other `%s` sign shows the date.

The home page

The home page contains variables to show the header part, the left column part, the right column part, the content top part, the content bottom part, and the footer part. Let's see how they are managed.

Go to `catalog/view/theme/packttheme/template/common/` and open `home.tpl`. You will see the following code:

```php
<?php echo $header; ?>
<div class="container">
  <div class="row"><?php echo $column_left; ?>
    <?php if ($column_left && $column_right) { ?>
    <?php $class = 'col-sm-6'; ?>
    <?php } elseif ($column_left || $column_right) { ?>
    <?php $class = 'col-sm-9'; ?>
    <?php } else { ?>
    <?php $class = 'col-sm-12'; ?>
    <?php } ?>
    <div id="content" class="<?php echo $class; ?>"><?php echo
$content_top; ?><?php echo $content_bottom; ?></div>
    <?php echo $column_right; ?></div>
</div>
<?php echo $footer; ?>
```

The `<?php echo $header; ?>` code is used to show the header part wherever we wish. In most cases, the template (`.tpl`) file `<?php echo $header; ?>` is the first code to write, as we show the header at the top.

Likewise, for the left column to be shown, we have to use `<?php echo $column_left; ?>`. The left column will be seen only when there is an activated module in it. Similarly, for the right column, we write `<?php echo $column_right; ?>`. The right column is also seen only when there is activated module in it. The `<?php echo $content_top; ?>` code shows the module just below the top category menu and between the columns if the columns are activated. Similarly, `<?php echo $content_bottom; ?>` shows the module just above the footer.

You can see there is no extra code in the home page except the modules shown.

So, you should always know after which div to show the modules in the top, left, right and bottom. When designing an OpenCart theme, we should take these four scenarios into consideration:

- One for the left column activated only
- Another is for the right column activated only
- Third for no column activated (only content)
- The last three column structure (left column, content section, and right column activated)

In OpenCart 2, it is controlled like this:

```php
<?php if ($column_left && $column_right) { ?>
    <?php $class = 'col-sm-6'; ?>
  <?php } elseif ($column_left || $column_right) { ?>
    <?php $class = 'col-sm-9'; ?>
  <?php } else { ?>
    <?php $class = 'col-sm-12'; ?>
  <?php } ?>
```

If both column left and column right are activated, then `col-sm-6` is shown for the content; if either column left or column right is activated, then `col-sm-9` is shown; and if there is neither column left nor column right, then `col-sm-12` is shown.

When we activate the **Category** module in the left column of the home page and the **Affiliate** module in the right column, the home page will look like what is shown in this screenshot:

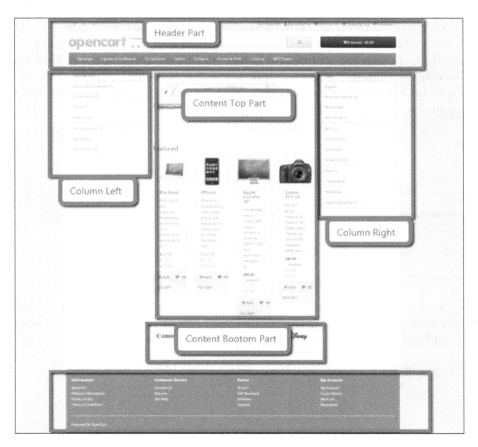

Let's do some settings to create three columns in the home page:

1. First, let's check whether the **Affiliate** module and the **Category** module are installed or not, For this go to **Administrator | Extensions | Modules** and find the **Affiliate** module. For a default setting it is not installed, so let's install it by clicking on the green **+** button, as shown in the following screenshot:

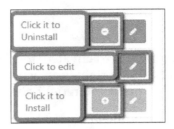

2. Then click on the blue edit button, choose the **Enabled** option, and save it. After this, go to the layout page to insert the module for the home page. You can go directly by clicking on the link in the message, or by going to **Administrator | System | Design | Layout** and finding the home page. Edit it, click on the add button in the module section, choose **Affiliate** for the module, position right, and input sort order equal to **1**. Again, click on the add button. Choose the **Category** module, position left, and input sort order equal to **1**. Then you will see this:

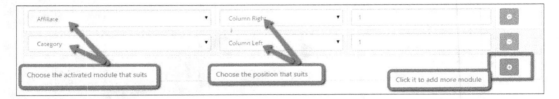

3. Next, click on save and refresh the home page.

In this way, we will see the three columns in the home page.

So, keep in mind that you should take care of the layout and position to show the modules in the correct position. In this way, you can make changes to any place you like and get the required changes to the default theme.

Let's now define the code for each page, starting with the category page.

The category page

In this section, we will describe the code of the category page.

Hover over **Desktops**, which shows a dropdown, and click on the **See All Desktops** category link in the top menu. You will see something like this:

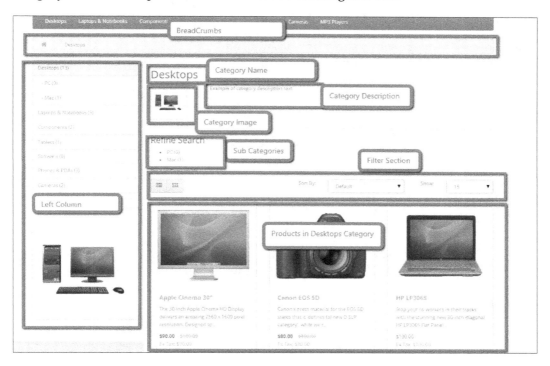

Now go to `catalog/view/theme/default/template` and copy the `product` folder. Then go to `catalog/view/theme/packttheme/template` and paste the `product` folder there. We have done this because we are going to change some things in the `product` folder's files, such as `category.tpl`, `product.tpl`, `search.tpl`. You should always create a copy of the files to which you wish to make the changes. After creating the copy, open `catalog/view/theme/packttheme/template/product/category.tpl`. You will see the following code, which we will describe now:

```php
<?php echo $header; ?><?php echo $column_left; ?><?php echo $column_right; ?>
```

As we've discussed already, `<?php echo $header; ?>` is used to show the header part, `<?php echo $column_left; ?>` is used to show the left column section, and `<?php echo $column_right; ?>` is used to show the right column section. So, you can insert this wherever you like to show the header, left column, and right column. Right now, we are just focusing the default design, so there are no changes in the div. Sometimes, there can be a custom design, and we have to show the column left and column right in a different div to look similar.

The following code is used to show breadcrumb, and the `$breadcrumbs` array holds the breadcrumb separator to separate the breadcrumb as `$breadcrumb['separator']` and the breadcrumb page link as `$breadcrumb['href']` and the breadcrumb text to show by `$breadcrumb['text']`. So, to show the breadcrumb, you should use this code:

```
<div class="container">
  <ul class="breadcrumb">
    <?php foreach ($breadcrumbs as $breadcrumb) { ?>
    <li><a href="<?php echo $breadcrumb['href']; ?>"><?php echo
$breadcrumb['text']; ?></a></li>
    <?php } ?>
  </ul>
```

The `id="content"` div is the content section, and the class value is given by the `$class` variable, which is given dynamically as per the column left and column right modules. The `<?php echo $content_top; ?>` code is used to show the top section modules:

```
<div class="row">
    <?php echo $column_left; ?>
    <?php if ($column_left && $column_right) { ?>
    <?php $class = 'col-sm-6'; ?>
    <?php } elseif ($column_left || $column_right) { ?>
    <?php $class = 'col-sm-9'; ?>
    <?php } else { ?>
    <?php $class = 'col-sm-12'; ?>
    <?php } ?>
    <div id="content" class="<?php echo $class; ?>"><?php echo
$content_top; ?>
```

The following code shows the category name in `category.tpl`:

```
<h1><?php echo $heading_title; ?></h1>
```

The following line of code is used to check whether there is an image and a description of the category:

```
<?php if ($thumb || $description) { ?>
```

The next code snippet is used to check whether there is a thumbnail or image of the category. If there is an image inserted in the category, then only it will show the image. Its `alt` tag has the category name, and `$heading_title` consists of the category name. The category image is adjustable from the admin, so when designing the theme, we must be sure that the images can be customized. Use the customized height and width in the documentation of the theme:

```
<?php if ($thumb) { ?>
  <div class="col-sm-2"><img src="<?php echo $thumb; ?>" alt="<?php
echo $heading_title; ?>" title="<?php echo $heading_title; ?>"
class="img-thumbnail" /></div>
<?php } ?>
```

It is the description of the category that we input while inserting the category details by going to **Administrator** | **Catalog** | **Categories**:

```
<?php if ($description) { ?>
        <div class="col-sm-10"><?php echo $description; ?></div>
<?php } ?>
```

The following code is used to check whether there are subcategories in the active category or not:

```
<?php if ($categories) { ?>
```

The next line of code will show the **Refine Search** text from the language file:

```
<h3><?php echo $text_refine; ?></h3>
```

The following code shows the subcategories of the active category. The code is written in such a way that if there are more than five categories, it starts showing the categories in columns:

```
<?php if (count($categories) <= 5) { ?>
  <div class="row">
    <div class="col-sm-3">
      <ul>
        <?php foreach ($categories as $category) { ?>
        <li><a href="<?php echo $category['href']; ?>"><?php echo
$category['name']; ?></a></li>
        <?php } ?>
      </ul>
```

```
    </div>
  </div>
  <?php } else { ?>
    <div class="row">
      <?php foreach (array_chunk($categories, ceil(count($categories)
/ 4)) as $categories) { ?>
      <div class="col-sm-3">
        <ul>
          <?php foreach ($categories as $category) { ?>
          <li><a href="<?php echo $category['href']; ?>"><?php echo
$category['name']; ?></a></li>
          <?php } ?>
        </ul>
      </div>
      <?php } ?>
    </div>
  <?php } ?>
```

For example, when you click on the **MP3 Players** category, you will see the subcategories as follows:

Refine Search

- test 11 (0)
- test 12 (0)
- test 15 (0)
- test 16 (0)
- test 17 (0)

- test 18 (0)
- test 19 (0)
- test 20 (0)
- test 21 (0)
- test 22 (0)

- test 23 (0)
- test 24 (0)
- test 4 (0)
- test 5 (0)
- test 6 (0)

- test 7 (0)
- test 8 (0)
- test 9 (0)

While designing, we can use the following code to show only subcategories:

```
<?phpforeach ($categories as $category) { ?>
<a href="<?php echo $category['href']; ?>"><?php echo
$category['name']; ?></a>
<?php } ?>
```

The `$categories` array holds subcategories of the active category, `$category['href']` is the link to the category pages, and `$category['name']` is the category name.

The following line checks whether the active category has products or not:

```
<?php if ($products) { ?>

<p><a href="<?php echo $compare; ?>" id="compare-total"><?php echo
$text_compare; ?></a></p>
```

The code you just saw shows the **Product Compare (0)** text; **0** is the total count of products added to compare. While designing, don't forget to insert `id="compare-total"`, as it automatically reloads to refresh the number of comparing products.

It shows the List-Grid button. When clicking on the Grid button, the List button gets activated and the listing of products is changed to grid form, and vice-versa:

```
<div class="row">
  <div class="col-md-4">
    <div class="btn-group hidden-xs">
      <button type="button" id="list-view" class="btn btn-default"
data-toggle="tooltip" title="<?php echo $button_list; ?>"><i class="fa
fa-th-list"></i></button>
      <button type="button" id="grid-view" class="btn btn-default"
data-toggle="tooltip" title="<?php echo $button_grid; ?>"><i class="fa
fa-th"></i></button>
    </div>

  </div>

</div>
```

You can check out the following screenshot, which show the part of the category page:

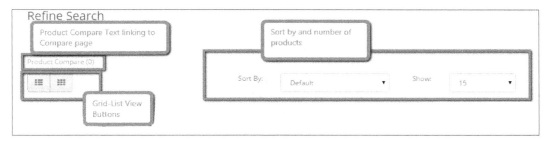

The following code shows the **Sort By:** text:

```
<div class="col-md-2 text-right">
  <label class="control-label" for="input-sort"><?php echo $text_sort;
?></label>
</div>
```

The next code snippet shows the select box for the sorting, and it consists of the sorting style of Name (A to Z), Name (Z to A), Price (Low to High), Price (High to Low), Rating (Highest), Rating (Lowest), Model (A to Z), and Model (Z to A). If you select among them, it sorts the products as per the selection:

```
<div class="col-md-3 text-right">
  <select id="input-sort" class="form-control" onchange="location =
this.value;">
```

```
    <?php foreach ($sorts as $sorts) { ?>
      <?php if ($sorts['value'] == $sort . '-' . $order) { ?>
        <option value="<?php echo $sorts['href']; ?>"
selected="selected"><?php echo $sorts['text']; ?></option>
      <?php } else { ?>
        <option value="<?php echo $sorts['href']; ?>"><?php echo
$sorts['text']; ?></option>
      <?php } ?><?php } ?>
    </select>
  </div>
```

The following code shows the **Show:** text:

```
<div class="col-md-1 text-right">
  <label class="control-label" for="input-limit"><?php echo $text_
limit; ?></label>
</div>
```

This code shows the drop-down box to limit the number of products to show per page. By default, it shows the number inserted at **Administrator | System | Setting** edit the active store and in the **Option** tab, the enter the number at *** Default Items Per Page (Catalog):**. The options provided are 25, 50, 75, and 100. This code determines the number of items to show per page:

```
<div class="col-md-2 text-right">
  <select id="input-limit" class="form-control" onchange="location =
this.value;">
    <?php foreach ($limits as $limits) { ?>
      <?php if ($limits['value'] == $limit) { ?>
        <option value="<?php echo $limits['href']; ?>"
selected="selected"><?php echo $limits['text']; ?></option>
      <?php } else { ?>
        <option value="<?php echo $limits['href']; ?>"><?php echo
$limits['text']; ?></option>
      <?php } ?>
    <?php } ?>
  </select>
  </div>
</div>
```

The following code is used to show products, and by default, products are shown in the grid in OpenCart 2:

```
<div class="row">
  <?php foreach ($products as $product) { ?>
    <div class="product-layout product-list col-xs-12">
```

The $products contains all the products of the active category:

```
<div class="product-thumb">
  <div class="image"><a href="<?php echo $product['href'];
?>"><img src="<?php echo $product['thumb']; ?>" alt="<?php echo
$product['name']; ?>" title="<?php echo $product['name']; ?>"
class="img-responsive" /></a></div>
<div>
```

If there is an image of the product, then it is shown, and the title and the alt tag of image are given the product name. If the product does not have an image, then it shows the default placeholder image from image/placeholder.png.

The following code is used to show the product's name and link to it. The name is given by $product['name'] and the link is given by $product['href']:

```
<div class="caption">
  <h4><a href="<?php echo $product['href']; ?>"><?php echo
$product['name']; ?></a></h4>
```

The next line of code is used to show the description of the product:

```
<p><?php echo $product['description']; ?></p>
```

The following code is used to show the rating, so you can use it if you wish to show the rating of the products in the **Category** page:

```
<?php if ($product['rating']) { ?>
<div class="rating">
  <?php for ($i = 1; $i <= 5; $i++) { ?>
  <?php if ($product['rating'] < $i) { ?>
  <span class="fa fa-stack"><i class="fa fa-star-o fa-
stack-2x"></i></span>
  <?php } else { ?>
  <span class="fa fa-stack"><i class="fa fa-star fa-
stack-2x"></i><i class="fa fa-star-o fa-stack-2x"></i></span>
  <?php } ?>
  <?php } ?>
</div>
<?php } ?>
```

This line of code is used to check whether the price needs to be shown or not. OpenCart supports hiding the price from the admin settings. So, it will show the price only when price showing is activated:

```
<?php if ($product['price']) { ?>
```

The following code is meant for showing the price. If a special price is not inserted, then it shows only the prices as shown in the image for the product **HP LP3056**. If a special price is inserted, then it shows the prices as shown for the **Canon EOS 5D** and the `price-old` class gives the strike and red color:

```
<p class="price">
  <?php if (!$product['special']) { ?>
    <?php echo $product['price']; ?>
                <?php } else { ?>
                <span class="price-new"><?php echo
$product['special']; ?></span> <span class="price-old"><?php echo
$product['price']; ?></span>
                <?php } ?>
```

You can use whichever design you like. One thing to remember is keep the special price and normal price:

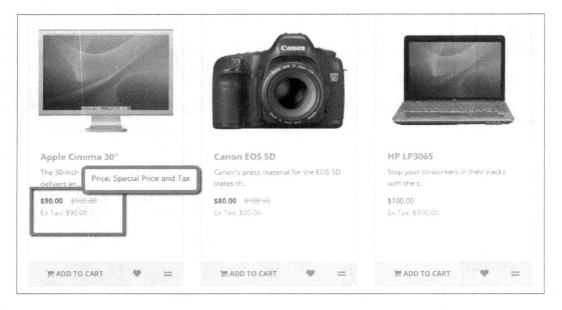

The following code is used to show the tax inserted for the product. As per the design management, the tax is shown only in the list view of products:

```
<?php if ($product['tax']) { ?>
  <span class="price-tax"><?php echo $text_tax; ?> <?php echo
$product['tax']; ?></span>
  <?php } ?>
</p>
                <?php } ?>
            </div>
```

The following code is used to show the add to cart button. While designing a new theme, if you use the default common.js, then the addToCart(product_id) function is used to add the product to the cart. So, in the category page, you can use onclick="addToCart('<?php echo $product['product_id']; ?>');", to add the product to the cart:

```
<div class="button-group">
  <button type="button" onclick="cart.add('<?php echo
$product['product_id']; ?>');">
    <i class="fa fa-shopping-cart"></i>
    <span class="hidden-xs hidden-sm hidden-md"><?php echo $button_
cart; ?>
    </span>
```

The following code shows the **Add to Wish List** functionality. When clicked, it adds the product to the wish list. We should take note of the addToWishList function which is defined in common.js:

```
<button type="button" data-toggle="tooltip" title="<?php echo $button_
wishlist; ?>" onclick="wishlist.add('<?php echo $product['product_
id']; ?>');">
  <i class="fa fa-heart"></i>
</button>
```

This code shows the **Add to Compare** button. It functions like add to cart and add to wishlist. When clicked, it adds the products to the comparing list, and the products are listed in a grid view.

```
              <button type="button" data-toggle="tooltip" title="<?php
echo $button_compare; ?>" onclick="compare.add('<?php echo
$product['product_id']; ?>');">
                <i class="fa fa-exchange"></i>
              </button>
            </div>
          </div>
        </div>
      </div>
  <?php } ?>
</div>
```

Here is a trick. We see the class of the list but the products are listed in a grid view, so the trick is done in the common.js file. The default listing is a grid view:

```
if (localStorage.getItem('display') == 'list') {
    $('#list-view').trigger('click');
} else {
    $('#grid-view').trigger('click');
}
```

Then, when a page loads by default, the class of the list is changed to the class of the grid:

```
<div class="row">
<div class="col-sm-6 text-left"><?php echo $pagination; ?></div>
<div class="col-sm-6 text-right"><?php echo $results; ?></div>
</div>
```

This code is used to show the pagination and resulting text, as shown in the following screenshot:

The preceding code checks whether there are products, and if not, it shows the **There are no products to list in this category.** message using `<?php echo $text_empty; ?>`.

```
<?php if (!$categories && !$products) { ?>
  <p><?php echo $text_empty; ?></p>
  <div class="buttons">
    <div class="pull-right"><a href="<?php echo $continue; ?>"
class="btn btn-primary"><?php echo $button_continue; ?></a>
    </div>
  </div>
<?php } ?>
```

When there are no products, the following message is shown with the **Continue** button:

The following code shows the `bottom` modules. So, you have to prepare the design to show the modules in the bottom sections as well:

```
<?php echo $content_bottom; ?>
```

The following JavaScript is meant to show the grid or list view of products. By default, products are shown in the grid view, and when clicking on the List button they are shown in the list view. You should take care of the CSS classes used if you are using the same JavaScript. Once clicked on, it gets stored in cookies and keeps on activating the view. Find the following JavaScript code to change the list-grid view of the product listing:

```
// Product List
  $('#list-view').click(function() {
    $('#content .product-layout > .clearfix').remove();
    $('#content .product-layout').attr('class', 'product-layout
product-list col-xs-12');
    localStorage.setItem('display', 'list');
  });
```

When the List button, which has `id="list-view"`, is clicked on, the `product-layout product-list col-xs-12` class is added for the product layout, and it shows the products in a list. The `localStorage` object stores the display data with no expiration date. The display data will not be deleted when the browser is closed, and will be available when we open it the next time:

```
// Product Grid
  $('#grid-view').click(function() {
    $('#content .product-layout > .clearfix').remove();
    // What a shame bootstrap does not take into account dynamically
loaded columns
    cols = $('#column-right, #column-left').length;
    if (cols == 2) {
      $('#content .product-layout').attr('class', 'product-layout
product-grid col-lg-6 col-md-6 col-sm-12 col-xs-12');
    } else if (cols == 1) {
      $('#content .product-layout').attr('class', 'product-layout
product-grid col-lg-4 col-md-4 col-sm-6 col-xs-12');
    } else {
      $('#content .product-layout').attr('class', 'product-layout
product-grid col-lg-3 col-md-3 col-sm-6 col-xs-12');
    }
    localStorage.setItem('display', 'grid');
  });
```

When the Grid button, which has `id="grid-view"`, is clicked on, the classes as per the column activated are selected and added for the product layout and the products are shown in a grid. If both the columns have modules, then it takes `class="product-layout product-grid col-lg-6 col-md-6 col-sm-12 col-xs-12"`; if only one column is activated, then it takes `class= "product-layout product-grid col-lg-4 col-md-4 col-sm-6 col-xs-12"`; and by default, it takes `class="'product-layout product-grid col-lg-3 col-md-3 col-sm-6 col-xs-12"`:

```
if (localStorage.getItem('display') == 'list') {
  $('#list-view').trigger('click');
} else {
  $('#grid-view').trigger('click');
}
```

When a page loads by default, the class of the list is changed to the class of the grid. When the display is set to list, the list view is shown:

```
<?php echo $footer; ?>
```

This code is used to show the footer part in the category page.

Other pages, such as the search results page, are also somewhat similar. Although, some changes are found in the search form so that you will be able to integrate the design with the search page as well. Similarly, in the special products' display page, you will be able to integrate the design, as it is similar to the category page. The manufacturer information products' listing page is also like the category page.

The product page

In the product page, we get detailed information about the product. Hover over the **Desktops** category menu and click on See All Desktops. You will get a list of desktop products. You can click on any one of them. Let's click on **Apple Cinema 30**, as it contains more details than other products. It contains a main image, additional images, a product name, a brand name, a product code, reward points, availability, a price, tax, options of the products such as the add to cart button, reviews, description of the product, specifications, and related products. Go to `catalog/view/theme/packttheme/template/product` and open `product.tpl`. We will describe only what we have not covered previously.

The $heading_title variable shows the name of the product, $thumb gives the URL path of the main image, and $popup gives the URL path of the pop-up image. When we click on this image, it pops up with Magnific Popup. The $images variable holds additional images, $tab_description shows the **Description** text, $tab_attribute shows the **Specification** text, and $tab_review shows the **Reviews** text with the number of reviews.

The $description variable shows the description of the product, the $attribute_groups variable holds the attributes of the product, and $review_status gives the status, that is, whether the review section is active or not, as we can disable the review section from an admin account. The $review_guest variable shows the status whether a guest or visitor is allowed to review without logging in:

```
    <button type="button" data-toggle="tooltip" class="btn btn-default"
title="<?php echo $button_wishlist; ?>" onclick="wishlist.add('<?php
echo $product_id; ?>');"><i class="fa fa-heart"></i></button>
    <button type="button" data-toggle="tooltip" class="btn btn-default"
title="<?php echo $button_compare; ?>" onclick="compare.add('<?php
echo $product_id; ?>');"><i class="fa fa-exchange"></i></button>
```

These code snippets show the wish list button and compare button just above the product name. See onclick="wishlist.add('<?php echo $product_id; ?>');" code on the click event of the wish list button, which adds the product to the wish list basket, and onclick="compare.add('<?php echo $product_id; ?>');" on the click event of the compare button, which adds the product to the compare table. So, while designing the theme, take these things into consideration.

The $manufacturer variable shows the manufacturer of the product, $model shows the model, $reward shows the points that the buyers can earn, and $stock shows the availability status. The $price variable shows the price, $special gives the special price, $tax gives the tax on the product, and $points shows the total number of points for which customers can buy this product.

The $discounts variable shows the discount that customer can get on a bulk purchase, and $options give the product options that the admin inserted while inserting the product information. The option type can be a select field, radio field, checkbox, image type, text field, text area field, file field, date field, date and time field, or time field. Each field will have an option name, its product option ID, and a status to check whether the option is required or not. The $recurrings variable shows the recurring payment option for paying for the product only when it is enabled for the product:

```
    <input type="text" name="quantity" value="<?php echo $minimum; ?>"
size="2" id="input-quantity" class="form-control" />
```

The preceding code shows the quantity input field:

```
<input type="hidden" name="product_id" value="<?php echo $product_
id; ?>" />
```

The code you just saw is used to pass the product ID without showing it in the product detail page:

```
<button type="button" id="button-cart" data-loading-text="<?php echo
$text_loading; ?>" class="btn btn-primary btn-lg btn-block"><?php echo
$button_cart; ?></button>
```

The preceding code is used to show the add to cart button, taking `id="button-cart"` into consideration, as JavaScript is written to add the product to the cart when the `button-cart` ID is clicked on:

```
<!-- AddThis Button BEGIN -->
        <div class="addthis_toolbox addthis_default_style"><a
class="addthis_button_facebook_like" fb:like:layout="button_count"></
a> <a class="addthis_button_tweet"></a> <a class="addthis_button_
pinterest_pinit"></a> <a class="addthis_counter addthis_pill_style"></
a></div>
        <script type="text/javascript" src="//s7.addthis.com/
js/300/addthis_widget.js#pubid=ra-515eeaf54693130e"></script>
```

This code is used to show the social media buttons: the Facebook **Like** button, **Tweet**, **Pin it**, and other sharing buttons.

The `$products` variable holds related products, and `$tags` holds the tags of the product and the link for the tags. The product page also includes JavaScript code used to retrieve the recurring description, the add to cart button-click script, date picker, file upload, review pagination code, review load, and the review button-click and Magnific Popup scripts.

The information pages

The information pages are made when information is inserted from **Information** which can be found by going to **Administration | Catalog**.

Now go to `catalog/view/theme/default/template/`, copy the `information` folder, and paste it in `catalog/view/theme/packttheme/template`. Open the `information` folder and then open `information.tpl` where you will see the following code. We have removed the code already described in the home and category pages:

```
<?php echo $header; ?>
  <div class="container">
```

```
<ul class="breadcrumb">
  <?php foreach ($breadcrumbs as $breadcrumb) { ?>
    <li><a href="<?php echo $breadcrumb['href']; ?>"><?php echo
$breadcrumb['text']; ?></a></li>
  <?php } ?>
</ul>
<div class="row"><?php echo $column_left; ?>
  <?php if ($column_left && $column_right) { ?>
  <?php $class = 'col-sm-6'; ?>
  <?php } elseif ($column_left || $column_right) { ?>
  <?php $class = 'col-sm-9'; ?>
  <?php } else { ?>
  <?php $class = 'col-sm-12'; ?>
  <?php } ?>
  <div id="content" class="<?php echo $class; ?>"><?php echo
$content_top; ?>
    <h1><?php echo $heading_title; ?></h1>
    <?php echo $description; ?><?php echo $content_bottom; ?>
  </div>
  <?php echo $column_right; ?></div>
</div>
<?php echo $footer; ?>
```

The `<h1><?php echo $heading_title; ?></h1>` is the information title that we inserted while inserting the information, and `<?php echo $description; ?>` is the information description. The rest of the code is used to show the **Continue** button, and everything else has been described already. You can change the styles of the information pages as per your requirement.

The contact us page

The contact us page shows the form used to send message to the administrator of the site. Now, go to `catalog/view/theme/packttheme/template/information/` and open `contact.tpl`. The following line of code shows the contact us title and is taken from the `catalog/language/english/information/contact.php` language file:

```
<h1><?php echo $heading_title; ?></h1>
```

The following line of code shows the location text:

```
<h3><?php echo $text_location; ?></h3>
```

The following code displays the image:

```php
<?php if ($image) { ?>
     <div class="col-sm-3"><img src="<?php echo $image; ?>"
alt="<?php echo $store; ?>" title="<?php echo $store; ?>" class="img-
thumbnail" /></div>
<?php } ?>
```

The following screenshot shows how an image can be set:

The following code shows the store name, store address and a Google Map as per the geographical code provided in our store settings:

```
<div class="col-sm-3"><strong><?php echo $store; ?></strong><br />
  <address>
    <?php echo $address; ?>
  </address>
<?php if ($geocode) { ?>
  <a href="https://maps.google.com/maps?q=<?php echo
urlencode($geocode); ?>&hl=en&t=m&z=15" target="_blank" class="btn
btn-info"><i class="fa fa-map-marker"></i> <?php echo $button_map;
?></a>
  <?php } ?>
</div>
```

The following code shows the telephone and fax numbers of the store:

```
<div class="col-sm-3">
  <strong><?php echo $text_telephone; ?></strong><br>
  <?php echo $telephone; ?><br />
    <br />
    <?php if ($fax) { ?>
      <strong><?php echo $text_fax; ?></strong><br>
    <?php echo $fax; ?>
  <?php } ?>
</div>
```

The following code shows the opening time details and the comment that we inserted in our store settings:

```
<div class="col-sm-3">
  <?php if ($open) { ?>
    <strong><?php echo $text_open; ?></strong><br />
    <?php echo $open; ?><br />
      <br />
    <?php } ?>
    <?php if ($comment) { ?>
      <strong><?php echo $text_comment; ?></strong><br />
    <?php echo $comment; ?>
  <?php } ?>
</div>
```

In OpenCart 2, we are able to show multiple store locations, and this is made possible by the `$locations` variable. We can insert a location by navigating to **Administrator | System | Localisation | Store Location**. Here, we can insert details such as store name, address, geocode, telephone, fax, image of the store, opening times, and comments about that store. In this way, we can show multiple store locations in the **Contact us** page:

```
<form action="<?php echo $action; ?>" method="post"
enctype="multipart/form-data" class="form-horizontal">
```

The starting code of the form, upon rendering the PHP, looks like this:

```
<form action="http://www.example.com/index.php?route=information/
contact" method="post" enctype="multipart/form-data">
```

This means that the form has been submitted to the controller `information/contact`:

The following line of code shows the contact us form text from the language file:

```
<h3><?php echo $text_contact; ?></h3>
```

The following code is used to show the **First Name** text and input box for first name:

```
<div class="form-group required">
  <label class="col-sm-2 control-label" for="input-name"><?php echo
$entry_name; ?></label>
  <div class="col-sm-10">
    <input type="text" name="name" value="<?php echo $name; ?>"
id="input-name" class="form-control" />
    <?php if ($error_name) { ?>
      <div class="text-danger"><?php echo $error_name; ?></div>
    <?php } ?>
  </div>
</div>
```

When you click on the **Continue** button on the contact us page, you will see an error just below the first name input box. It will look like this: **Name must be between 3 and 32 characters!**

The following code shows the **E-Mail Address**: text and, just below it, an input box for entering the e-mail address. When you submit the form, if the entered e-mail is not in the e-mail format or the input box is empty, an error is shown by the following error code:

```
<div class="form-group required">
  <label class="col-sm-2 control-label" for="input-email"><?php echo
$entry_email; ?></label>
```

```
    <div class="col-sm-10">
      <input type="text" name="email" value="<?php echo $email; ?>"
id="input-email" class="form-control" />
      <?php if ($error_email) { ?>
        <div class="text-danger"><?php echo $error_email; ?></div>
      <?php } ?>
    </div>
  </div>
```

The code that is up next is used to show the **Enquiry:** text and the text area required to enter the content to submit. If the enquiry length is small, then it shows an error:

```
<div class="form-group required">
  <label class="col-sm-2 control-label" for="input-enquiry"><?php echo
$entry_enquiry; ?></label>
  <div class="col-sm-10">
    <textarea name="enquiry" rows="10" id="input-enquiry" class="form-
control"><?php echo $enquiry; ?></textarea>
      <?php if ($error_enquiry) { ?>
    <div class="text-danger"><?php echo $error_enquiry; ?></div>
    <?php } ?>
  </div>
</div>
```

The following code shows the **Enter the code in the box below:** text. This is the input box required to enter the CAPTCHA:

```
<div class="form-group required">
  <label class="col-sm-2 control-label" for="input-captcha"><?php echo
$entry_captcha; ?></label>
  <div class="col-sm-10">
    <input type="text" name="captcha" id="input-captcha" class="form-
control" />
  </div>
</div>
```

The following code displays an active CAPTCHA:

```
      <div class="form-group">
        <div class="col-sm-10 pull-right">
        <img src="index.php?route=tool/captcha" alt="" />
          <?php if ($error_captcha) { ?>
            <div class="text-danger">
          <?php echo $error_captcha; ?>
        </div>
        <?php } ?>
      </div>
    </div>
```

When the entered CAPTCHA and active CAPTCHA do not match, it will show an error. This CAPTCHA code is for versions older than OpenCart 2.0.2.0. From 2.0.2.0 onwards, OpenCart uses Google **reCAPTCHA**. You can learn more about Google reCAPTCHA from `https://developers.google.com/recaptcha/`. We need to register for this website, so go to `https://www.google.com/recaptcha/admin` and insert the label and website URL. Click on the **Register** button and get the site key and secret key. Now, go to **Administrator | System | Settings** and edit your store. Go to the **Google** tab and insert the site key and secret key of Google reCAPTCHA.

This screenshot shows where to insert the site key and secret key of Google reCAPTCHA:

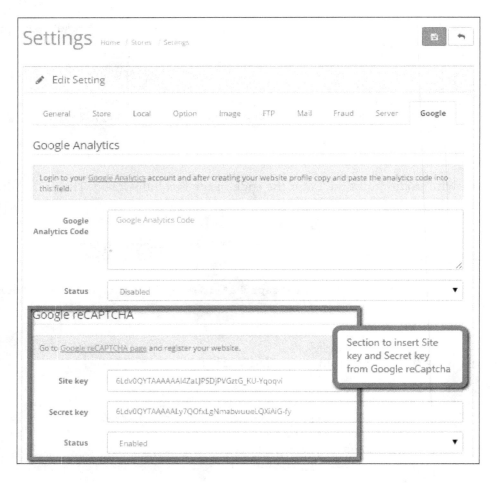

So, to show the CAPTCHA on the **Contact us** page in the view section, the following code has to be written:

```php
<?php if ($site_key) { ?>
  <div class="form-group">
    <div class="col-sm-offset-2 col-sm-10">
      <div class="g-recaptcha" data-sitekey="<?php echo $site_key;
?>"></div>
      <?php if ($error_captcha) { ?>
        <div class="text-danger"><?php echo $error_captcha; ?></div>
      <?php } ?>
    </div>
  </div>
<?php } ?>
```

In this code, `$site_key` is a variable that is used to check whether the Google reCAPTCHA site key is inserted or not in the admin section. If Google reCAPTCHA's site key is inserted in the admin, then it adds the following code to the JavaScript view section:

```
<script src="https://www.google.com/recaptcha/api.js" type="text/
javascript"></script>
```

The reCAPTCHA is shown at:

```php
<div class="g-recaptcha" data-sitekey="<?php echo $site_key; ?>"></
div>
```

The following code shows the **Continue** button and, upon clicking on it, submits the contact us form:

```php
<div class="buttons">
  <div class="pull-right">
    <input class="btn btn-primary" type="submit" value="<?php echo
$button_submit; ?>" />
  </div>
</div>
```

This is the closure of the form:

```
</form>
```

Like this, the **Contact us** page is formed, so we need to take care of input boxes and errors while designing a new theme.

Changing the CSS for the checkout steps

We will now change the style of the checkout steps, as shown in this screenshot:

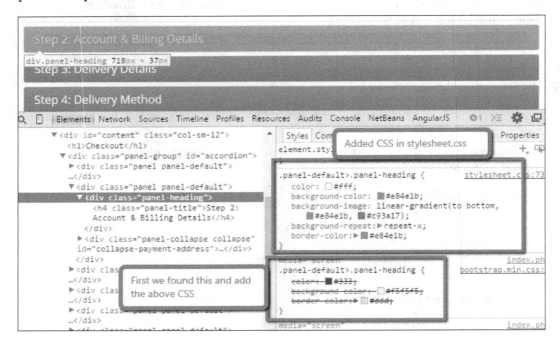

We inspect the element, as shown in the following screenshot, and change the CSS as per our requirement:

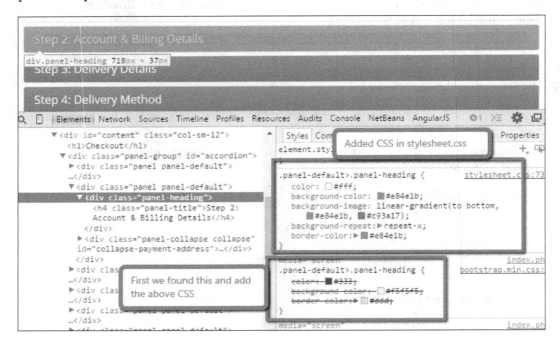

Add the following CSS to the end of `catalog/view/theme/packttheme/stylesheet/stylesheet.css` and refresh the checkout steps. You will see the changes. You can see the canceled portion of CSS from `bootstrap.min.css`, which means that the `bootstrap.min.css` class is overridden by the `stylesheet.css` class:

```
.panel-default>.panel-heading {
  color: #fff;
  background-color:#e84e1b;
background-image: linear-gradient(to bottom, #e84e1b, #c93a17);
  background-repeat: repeat-x;
  border-color: #e84e1b;
}
```

The code has changed the step's heading to an orange background. In this way, you can make changes and implement them in your theme.

Summary

In this chapter, we listed the checklist of things to take into consideration when creating the header, footer, and other sections as we created a new custom theme. After that, we changed the style of the currency module and showed it in a row style. Then we described the code of the top category menu and styled the top menu with different CSS. Likewise, we changed the style of the buttons and the footer box and removed the copyright.

We described most of the content area code, such as that of the home page, the category page, the information pages, and the contact us page. Likewise, we edited CSS in a style sheet to change the background. With this knowledge, you will be able to customize themes and create new designs for them. In the next chapter, we will discuss OpenCart modules.

4
Getting Started with OpenCart 2 Modules

OpenCart is an e-commerce cart application built with its own in-house framework, which uses the MVCL pattern. Thus, each module in OpenCart also follows the MVCL pattern. The controller creates logic and gathers data from the model. It passes this data to display it in the View. In this chapter, we will deal with the following topics:

- Creating a `Hello World` module.
- Defining OpenCart modules `admin` and `catalog` folders and file code in the `admin` folder helps control the setting of the module, and files in the `catalog` folder handle the presentation layer (frontend).
- Each module has its own files, because of which it becomes modular, and changing one module's file does not affect other modules. In OpenCart 2, we can create multiple instances of one module and have a dynamic module name. Modules do not hold the layout; rather, the layout holds the modules, which are made more modular.

With one module, we can create many modules and show them as different modules. For example, we can install the Featured module, edit it, and insert the module name as `Featured Products`. Then we select the products as required; enter `limit`, `width`, and `height` for the image; and select the status. Then, after we've clicked on save, it will create a new submodule of `Featured Products`. So, we can create any number of featured products modules and give each a different module name. For example, for the `Featured Products` in another instance, we can give it another name, say `Hot Products`. This makes OpenCart 2 an unlimited module instance system.

Creating a Hello World module

You are going to create a `Hello World` module. It has one input field for the heading title and another description text area for the details. The first step in module creation is using a unique name so that there will be no conflict with other modules. The same unique name is used to create the filename and class name to extend the controller and model.

There are generally six to eight files that need to be created for each module, and they follow a similar structure. If there is an interaction with database tables, then we have to create two extra models. The following screenshot shows the hierarchy of files and folders for an OpenCart module:

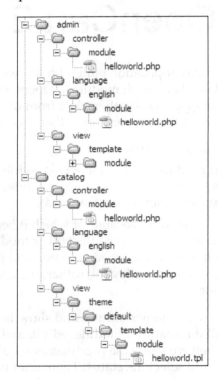

So now you know the basic directory structure of an OpenCart module. The file structure is divided into two sections: admin and catalog. The folders and files in the admin section deal with the settings of modules and data handling, while the folders and files in the catalog folder handle the frontend presentation. We will now create a Hello World module by cloning an existing HTML module. This will show you how a module works and how files and folders are created.

 In *Chapter 5, Extensions Code*, and *Chapter 6, Create OpenCart Custom Pages*, we've described each piece of code so that you will be able to create a custom module from scratch.

For rapid development, it is easy to clone an existing module by adding or removing the required element. For example, if we need to work on something with products, then we can clone the latest module. If we have to select products and display them, then we can use the Featured module. Now, to create an input box and a description field, we can clone the HTML Content module.

The admin folder

Let's make the following changes to the admin folder:

1. Go to admin/controller/module. Copy html.php and paste it in the same folder. Rename it as helloworld.php and open it in your favorite text editor. Then find the following lines:

   ```
   class ControllerModuleHTML extends Controller {
   ```

   Change the class name to this:

   ```
   class ControllerModuleHelloworld extends Controller {
   ```

2. Now find html and replace all its occurrences with helloworld. Then save the file.

3. Go to admin/language/english/module. Copy html.php and paste it in the same folder. Rename it to helloworld.php and open it. Then find HTML Content and replace all its occurrences with Hello World. Next save the file.

4. Go to admin/view/template/module. Copy html.tpl and paste it in the same folder. Rename it to helloworld.tpl.

The catalog folder

Let's make the following changes to the `catalog` folder:

1. Go to `catalog/controller/module`. Copy `html.php` and paste it in the same folder. Rename it to `helloworld.php`, open it, and find the following line:

    ```
    class ControllerModuleHTML extends Controller {
    ```

    Change the class name to this:

    ```
    class ControllerModuleHelloworld extends Controller {
    ```

2. Then find `$data['html']` and replace it with `$data['helloworld']`. Likewise, find `html.tpl` and replace it with `helloworld.tpl`. Click on the blue (save) button.

3. Finally, go to `catalog/view/theme/default/template/module` and copy the `html.tpl` file. Paste it in the same folder and rename it to `helloworld.tpl`. Then open it, find `$html`, replace it with `$helloworld`, and click on the blue (save) button.

4. With these file and code changes, our `helloworld` module is ready to install:

5. Now log in to the **Administration** section and go to **Extension | Module**. Then find the **Hello World** module and click on the green (install) button. Next click on the blue (edit) button:

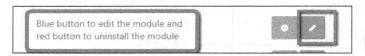

6. Then you will see a form like the one shown in the following screenshot. There, you have to enter for the **Hello World** module's content:

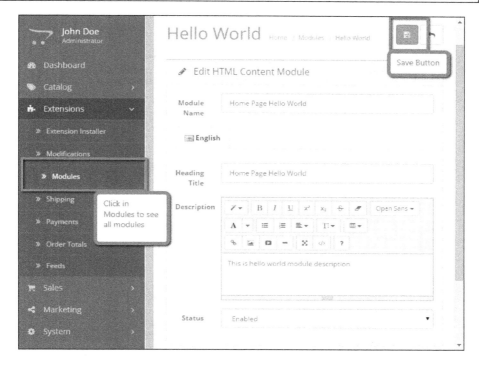

7. Enter the module name that is used in the layout section, content heading title, and description. Choose **Enabled** as the status and then click on the blue (save) button. Next go to the layout section. One way of doing this is by clicking on the link given in the module section, as shown in this screenshot:

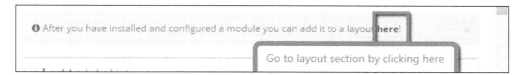

8. The other way is by navigating through the menu **Administrator | System | Design | Layouts**. Then click on the blue (edit) button of the layout where you want to show the module. We have planned to show the module on the home page, so let's click on the blue (edit) button of **Home**, as shown here:

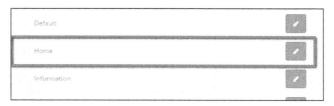

9. You will then see a form like this:

10. You can enter a name for the layout, routes for different stores, and modules to show for that page. To add our `Hello World` module, we click on the last blue button (add module). In the **Module** column, select **Hello World > Home Page Hello World Module Name**; in the **Position** column, select **Column Left**; and in the **Sort Order** field, enter **1**. Then click on the blue (save) button.

With these settings for the module, the `Hello World` module will be on the Home page, and it will be shown in the left column, as per the position we set, as the status is enabled.

Now go to the frontend of the site and open the home page. Then you will see the `Hello World` module in the left column. The following is the list of files that you need to upload to your live server:

- `admin/language/english/module/helloworld.php`
- `admin/controller/module/helloworld.php`
- `admin/view/template/module/helloworld.tpl`
- `catalog/controller/module/helloworld.php`
- `catalog/view/theme/default/template/module/helloworld.tpl`

After uploading these files, installing the module, and providing the settings, your `Hello World` module is ready for use.

You can change the `Hello World` text to whatever you like, such as `Welcome to our Store`, by typing the welcome message in the `Hello World` module's content while setting up the module. You can also show the welcome message at the frontend.

Installing, configuring, and uninstalling a module

There are many default modules in OpenCart. How are modules installed? Which are the database tables that hold the settings for a module? These are really questions for developers, and they will help them understand the structure and workings of modules.

Installing a module

Follow these instructions to install modules:

1. Go to **Administrator | Extensions | Modules**. There you will find a list of modules. Just click on the green (install) button and the module will be installed.

2. When you click on the green (install) button, the `extension/module` controller's `install` function is called. Now open `admin/controller/extension/module.php`. You will see the `public function install()`, which performs the permission check. If you get a **Permission Denied!** message, as shown in the following screenshot, then refer to the next step:

3. You have to provide access permission by going to **Administrator** | **User** | **User Group**. Then edit the user group name (in the following screenshot, we are editing Administrator), check the `module/extension`, and provide permission to access and modify so that you will be able to edit the modules. If you check only access, then you can only view it; you cannot edit or modify it. If you check both access and modify, then you can view and edit the module settings.

4. If you are provided with access, the `install()` function from `admin/model/setting/extension.php` is loaded.

```
$this->model_extension_extension->install('module', $this->request->get['extension']);
```

5. This means that data is inserted into the `oc_extension` table (where `oc_` is the prefix used during the installation of OpenCart) of the database with `type=module`, and `code=helloworld` in the case of our `Hello World` module. You can view the added data in the database using phpMyAdmin, or another database tool. It may be shown like this:

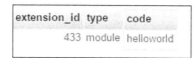

Configuring the module

Configuring the module means inserting the values or settings for the module:

1. After you've clicked on the green (install) button of the module, the red (uninstall) button and the blue (edit) button get activated. After clicking on the blue (edit) button, you will see the form where you have to enter data for the module. The Hello World module's content is saved in the oc_module table of the database.

2. Every module has a name, code, and set data. Set data is inserted in the setting row of the oc_module table, and saved in the serialized array. If the value of the input field of the form is in an array, then the value is saved with serialize($value). The serialize() method of PHP generates a storable representation of a value for an array. Likewise, we can convert them back using unserialize(), which takes a single serialized variable and converts it back to a PHP value.

For more information, you can visit http://php.net/manual/en/function.serialize.php.

Configuring layouts for the module

OpenCart has default page layouts that are based on the route of the page. Some layouts can be found by navigating to **Admininstrator | System | Design | Layouts**. They are **Account, Affiliate, Category, Checkout, Contact, Default, Home, Information, Manufacturer, Product**, and **Sitemap**.

Now edit one of them; let's take **Account**. You will see something like this:

The value of **Route** is `account/%`, which means that the module will be seen where the route value contains `account`. If your URL is `http://example.com/index.php?route=account/login`, then the module is shown as `route=account`. If you want to show the module in the account section, then you have to choose the layout as `Account`. If you wish to show the module in the affiliate section, then you have to choose the `Affiliate` layout, as the route of `Affiliate` is `route=affiliate` in the URL. Similarly, for other layouts, routes can be found at **Administrator | System | Setting | Design | Layouts | Edit**. See the `route` and check out the URL route. You will find out where the module will show up on choosing the layout name.

Uninstalling the module

If you don't need the installed module, then you can uninstall it with the help of the following instructions:

Go to **Administrator | Extensions | Modules**. There you will find the list of modules. Just click on the red (uninstall) button. The module gets uninstalled and all the settings get deleted.

Let's see how this is done: open `admin/controller/extension/module.php`. You will see `public function uninstall()` which performs the permission check, and if there is permission to access, it loads the model's `setting/extension` uninstall function.

Positions for the module

There are four positions for a module. They are as follows:

- Column Left
- Column Right
- Content Top
- Content Bottom

The following table shows the positions for a module in the frontend:

Header			
Content Left	**Content Top**		**Content Right**
	Main Content		
	Content Bottom		
Footer			

Choose the module position as per your requirement.

The status of the module

The status shows whether the module is enabled or disabled. If enabled, it is shown at the frontend, otherwise it is not.

Sort order of modules

If there is more than one module in any position, then the sort order plays its role. Let's suppose two modules, `Hello World` and `Account`, are positioned in the right column of the layout, and you want to show `Hello World` first. Then you want to show the `Account` module below it. So, you have to insert sort order as 1 for `Hello World` and 2 for `Account`. If you don't insert the sort order, then the Account module shows up at the top. Go to **Administration** | **System** | **Design** | **Layouts**. Then edit the `Account` layout and insert the details, as shown in the following screenshot:

Click on the blue (add module) button and choose the `Hello World` module in the **Module** section. Select **Column Right** as the position. Enter 1 as the **Sort Order** for `Hello World` and 2 as the **Sort Order** for `Account`. Now go to the home page and click on the **My Account** link. Go to the login page and you will see something like what is shown in the following screenshot—the `Hello World` module at the top and the `Account` module links below it:

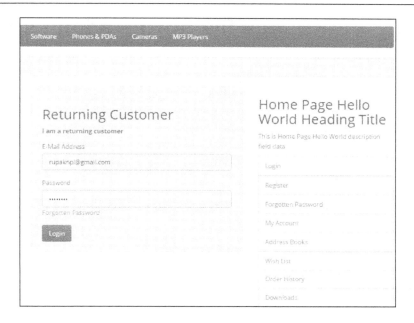

Different layouts for the same module

We can show the same module in a different layout. For this, go to **Administrator | System | Design | Layouts**, and click on the blue (edit) button where you want to show the module. For instance, if you want to show the `Hello World` module in the home page and the account page, then edit the **Home** layout, click on the blue (add module) button, and select the `Hello World` module in the **Module** column. Select the **Position** where you want to show the module, enter the value for **Sort Order**, and click on the blue (save) button. Likewise, we insert the `Hello World` module for the account page. Click on the blue (edit) button for the `Account` layout and then on the blue (add module) button. Another row will be added. Select the appropriate module, position and sort order. Then click on the blue (save) button and you will be able to see module in the respective layout.

The file structure – admin and frontend

When someone uses a module, then it is bound to have an admin section so that the administrator can handle the module functionality and customize the module's settings, such as position, layout, status, and sort order. By all of this, users can show the module wherever they like and enter the customized data that is needed for the module.

Creating a language file for the admin section in OpenCart

Language files are named as MODULENAME.php. For instance, let's say we want to create a language file for the Hello World module. We have to create a helloworld.php file. Language files use the constant=value configuration, where the constant name is used in the code, which never changes. Only the value for that language changes. If the English language is active, then the module retrieves the constant from the English language folder's file, and if some other language is active, then it retrieves the constant from the file of the other language's folder.

For example, for the English language, the constant is taken from the English language folder's file, like this:

```
$_['text_review'] = 'Product Review';
```

In some cases, language variables can use %s to indicate a text string that will be replaced in the controller using sprint for dynamic strings.

If the Spanish language is active, then the constant is taken from the Spanish language folder's file:

```
$_['text_review'] = 'De Revisión de Producto';
```

If the German language is active, the constant is taken from the German language folder's file:

```
$_['text_review'] = 'ProduktBewertung';
```

Within the file, we will assign each line of text to a variable as $_['variablename']. The same variablename will be used in the controller to access the text or messages. We should follow the standards that OpenCart uses to name a language variable to ensure that it does not conflict with any other variable. For example, a table column starts with column_; for normal text messages, it starts with text_; for errors, it starts with error_; and so on, shown as follows:

```
$data['heading_title'] = $this->language->get('heading_title');
```

Now, on the controller, we use heading_title to access the Hello World text.

If OpenCart cannot find a translated word for a particular variable in the user-chosen language, it will display such a word from the English folder in the language folder; so it is very important to add the English translation file, with all variables there, and your respective translated file into your language folder.

You can see the following code at `admin/language/english/module` in the `helloworld.php` file:

```php
<?php
// Heading
$_['heading_title']      = 'Hello World';
// Text
$_['text_module']        = 'Modules';
$_['text_success']       = 'Success: You have modified Hello World
module!';
$_['text_edit']          = 'Edit Hello World Module';
// Entry
$_['entry_name']         = 'Module Name';
$_['entry_title']        = 'Heading Title';
$_['entry_description']  = 'Description';
$_['entry_status']       = 'Status';
// Error
$_['error_permission']   = 'Warning: You do not have permission to
modify Hello World module!';
$_['error_name']         = 'Module Name must be between 3 and 64
characters!';
```

Creating a controller for the admin section in OpenCart

The controller controls the logic and data of the model where the variables for values and languages are set and passed to the presentation layer to display. A controller in OpenCart is simply a class file that is named in a way that can be associated with a URI. For example, in the `http://example.com/index.php?route=module/helloworld` URI, OpenCart will attempt to find a controller file called `helloworld.php` in the `module` folder with the class as `ControllerModuleHelloworld`.

We can see the code at `admin/controller/module/helloworld.php`, whose functionality is described in the next section.

In OpenCart, controller class names must start with the name of the controller and the folder in which the module is located, and the filename without extension. For example, in the `Hello World` module, the class name for the controller is `ControllerModuleHelloworld`, as it is inside the module folder and the filename is `helloworld.php`. Also, always make sure your controller extends the parent controller class:

```php
class ControllerModuleHelloworld extends Controller {
```

Whenever the controller is called, by default, the index method (`public function index()`) is always loaded.

The following line of code loads the language file variables of `helloworld.php`, which is in the module folder (`admin/language/*/module/helloworld.php`, where * represents the language folder). Now, you are able to get the text or messages by referring to the variable, like this: `$this->language->get('heading_title')`. This means that the `Hello World` text is ready to transfer to the template files:

```
$this->language->load('module/helloworld');
```

The following line of code sets the title of the document to Hello World:

```
$this->document->setTitle($this->language->get('heading_title'));
```

The line `$this->load->model('extension/module');` loads the `module.php` file of the `extension` folder, which is in the `model` folder. As before, it loads `module.php` located at `admin/model/extension`. Your module can load any model file in its controller file using the following code if they are in the same `admin` or `catalog` folder as the controller. You will need to specify the path to the file you want to load from the `admin` folder within parentheses. The preceding code will load the settings class so that we will have access to the functions within the `ModelExtensionModule` class in our model's controller file. Use the following format in your code to call a function from a loaded model file:

```
$this->model_extension_module->addModule('helloworld', $this->request-
>post);
if (($this->request->server['REQUEST_METHOD'] == 'POST') && $this-
>validate()) {
  if (!isset($this->request->get['module_id'])) {
    $this->model_extension_module->addModule('helloworld', $this-
>request->post);
  } else {
    $this->model_extension_module->editModule($this->request-
>get['module_id'], $this->request->post);
  }
  $this->session->data['success'] = $this->language->get('text_
success');
  $this->response->redirect($this->url->link('extension/module',
'token=' . $this->session->data['token'], 'SSL'));
}
```

When the form is saved in the module section, the preceding code, which is in `admin/controller/module/helloworld.php`, runs. If it is submitted through the POST and then validated, and the function returns `true`, only then are all the settings saved in the database, in the `oc_module` table. A success message is assigned to the success variable and is redirected to the list of module pages:

```
protected function validate() {
    if (!$this->user->hasPermission('modify', 'module/helloworld')){
    $this->error['warning'] = $this->language->get('error_permission');
    }
    if ((utf8_strlen($this->request->post['name']) < 3) || (utf8_
strlen($this->request->post['name']) > 64)) {
        $this->error['name'] = $this->language->get('error_name');
    }
    return !$this->error;
}
```

When the form is submitted, it is validated to determine whether permission is provided or not. It also checks whether the Hello World content consists of text or not. If no access is provided or no content is entered, then the error is returned true and it shows either `Module Name must be between 3 and 64 characters!` or `Permission Denied!`. It alerts the user to provide access or insert the content:

```
$data['heading_title'] = $this->language->get('heading_title');
$data['text_enabled'] = $this->language->get('text_enabled');
```

The `$this->language->get('heading_title')` line assigns the `Hello World` text of the `helloworld.php` language file, and from `$this->language->get('text_enabled')` the enabled text of the language file is assigned to `$data['text_enabled']`, and the same for the other:

```
if (isset($this->error['warning'])) {
    $data['error_warning'] = $this->error['warning'];
    } else {
      $data['error_warning'] = '';
    }
```

The `Hello World` module checks for the permission and shows a warning if the user does not have access to the module:

```
if (isset($this->error['name'])) {
    $data['error_name'] = $this->error['name'];
    } else {
      $data['error_name'] = '';
    }
```

If no content is inserted into the `Hello World` module's content field and the user tries to save the module, then it checks whether the content is inputted or not. If no content is inputted, then an error is activated and it will show the error as `Module Name must be between 3 and 64 characters!`:

```
$data['breadcrumbs'] = array();
$data['breadcrumbs'][] = array(
  'text' => $this->language->get('text_home'),
'href' => $this->url->link('common/dashboard', 'token=' . $this-
>session->data['token'], 'SSL')
);

$data['breadcrumbs'][] = array(
  'text' => $this->language->get('text_module'),
'href' => $this->url->link('extension/module', 'token=' . $this-
>session->data['token'], 'SSL')
);

if (!isset($this->request->get['module_id'])) {
  $data['breadcrumbs'][] = array(
    'text' => $this->language->get('heading_title'),
'href' => $this->url->link('module/helloworld', 'token=' . $this-
>session->data['token'], 'SSL')
  );

} else {
  $data['breadcrumbs'][] = array(
    'text' => $this->language->get('heading_title'),
'href' => $this->url->link('module/helloworld', 'token=' . $this-
>session->data['token'] . '&module_id=' . $this->request->get['module_
id'], 'SSL')
  );
}
```

The `breadcrumbs` array is defined and elements (text and link) are passed, and the same `breadcrumbs` array is used in the template files to show the text and link it:

```
if (!isset($this->request->get['module_id'])) {
  $data['action'] = $this->url->link('module/helloworld', 'token=' .
$this->session->data['token'], 'SSL');
} else {
$data['action'] = $this->url->link('module/helloworld', 'token='
. $this->session->data['token'] . '&module_id=' . $this->request-
>get['module_id'], 'SSL');
}
```

This will create a link which will be stored in the action variable. If we have to create a link in the admin area, then we need to use the preceding example. A token is used to preserve the admin user state:

```
$data['cancel'] = $this->url->link('extension/module', 'token=' .
$this->session->data['token'], 'SSL');
```

This will create a link that is stored in the cancel variable and is available in the template section.

OpenCart 2, supports unlimited module instance systems. Thus, the following code is used to check whether it is an already inserted module or a newly created module. If it is an already inserted module, then the module information is retrieved. It is checked with the module ID:

```
if (isset($this->request->get['module_id']) && ($this->request-
>server['REQUEST_METHOD'] != 'POST')) {
$module_info = $this->model_extension_module->getModule($this-
>request->get['module_id']);
}
```

This is used to check whether the module's heading title is already inserted, or if it is for the new module name or the form submitted module's heading title. The `if (isset($this->request->post['name']))` statement is used to check whether the form is submitted. If it is, then the module heading title is set as a submitted value. If we edit any instance of an already inserted module, then it is checked by `elseif (!empty($module_info))`. If it is an already inserted module, then the heading title is set as per the module inserted. Otherwise, the module heading title field is kept blank:

```
if (isset($this->request->post['name'])) {
    $data['name'] = $this->request->post['name'];
} elseif (!empty($module_info)) {
    $data['name'] = $module_info['name'];
} else {
    $data['name'] = '';
}
```

The following code is used to check for the description field:

```
if (isset($this->request->post['module_description'])) {
$data['module_description'] = $this->request->post['module_
description'];
} elseif (!empty($module_info)) {
$data['module_description'] = $module_info['module_description'];
```

```
  } else {
    $data['module_description'] = '';
  }
```

OpenCart supports multiple languages, so we can get a list of languages, as shown in the following code:

```
$this->load->model('localisation/language');
$data['languages'] = $this->model_localisation_language-
>getLanguages();
```

The following code is used to check for the status field:

```
if (isset($this->request->post['status'])){
  $data['status'] = $this->request->post['status'];
} elseif (!empty($module_info)){
  $data['status'] = $module_info['status'];
} else {
  $data['status'] = '';
}
```

The following code is used to load the header, column_left, and footer into the Hello World module. In the template section, we can use <?php echo $header; ?> to show the header section. The $this->response->setOutput() line sends data to the browser, whether it is HTML or JSON, and $data sends all of the data as a variable that is accessible at the template page:

```
$data['header'] = $this->load->controller('common/header');
$data['column_left'] = $this->load->controller('common/column_left');
$data['footer'] = $this->load->controller('common/footer');
$this->response->setOutput($this->load->view('module/helloworld.tpl',
$data));
```

Creating a template file for the admin section in OpenCart

We are creating the presentation or view section in admin for the OpenCart module, and we create a .tpl file for it. In the view section, we show the variable given by the controller and display it in the structure using HTML and CSS. As in the controller, $data['header'] is mapped as $header on the template.

Open the `admin/view/template/module/helloworld.tpl` file. We are describing the code, taking some snippets only. The `$header` and `$footer` variables are passed from the controller as the template's children:

```
<?php echo $header; ?>
<?php echo $footer; ?>
```

With this, the content of the `header` and `footer` are shown in the `module` section:

```
$data['header'] = $this->load->controller('common/header');
$data['footer'] = $this->load->controller('common/footer');
```

It shows the buttons used to `save` and `cancel`. Upon clicking on the `save` button, the form, with the ID `form-html`, is submitted. Upon clicking on `cancel`, it calls the `extension/module` controller, which means that it is redirected to the list of the modules:

```
<div class="pull-right">
<button type="submit" form="form-html" data-toggle="tooltip"
title="<?php echo $button_save; ?>" class="btn btn-primary"><i
class="fa fa-save"></i></button>
<a href="<?php echo $cancel; ?>" data-toggle="tooltip" title="<?php
echo $button_cancel; ?>" class="btn btn-default"><i class="fa fa-
reply"></i></a>
</div>
```

The following code shows the heading title passed from the controller as `$data['heading_title'] = $this->language->get('heading_title');`:

```
<h1><?php echo $heading_title; ?></h1>
```

The breadcrumbs section of the module

To keep a track of navigation `breadcrumbs` are used, and in the template file `breadcrumbs` are shown by the following lines of code:

```
<ul class="breadcrumb">
  <?php foreach ($breadcrumbs as $breadcrumb) { ?>
  <li>
    <a href="<?php echo $breadcrumb['href']; ?>"><?php echo
$breadcrumb['text']; ?></a>
  </li>
  <?php } ?>
</ul>
```

The `$breadcrumbs` array has now been passed by the controller files. It consists of the URI link and the text to be shown. All elements of the `breadcrumbs` array are managed in the controller:

```php
<?php if ($error_warning) { ?>
  <div class="alert alert-danger">
    <i class="fa fa-exclamation-circle"></i>
    <?php echo $error_warning; ?>
    <button type="button" class="close" data-dismiss="alert">&times;</
button>
  </div>
<?php } ?>
```

A warning will be shown if you have no permission to access or edit the module. As per the `Hello World` module, it checks for permission and shows a warning if the user does not have access to the module. The following screenshot shows the `breadcrumbs`, `header_title`, and save and cancel buttons:

The form code is started, and it has `id=form-html`, which is used in the save button to submit, when clicked, the save and action to the `module/helloworld` controller, which processes the submitted data:

```
<form action="<?php echo $action; ?>" method="post"
enctype="multipart/form-data" id="form-html" class="form-horizontal">
```

This is the module name field that shows the **Module Name** text by `$entry_name` and the input field used to enter the module name. If this input field is submitted empty, then it shows an error:

```
<div class="form-group">
  <label class="col-sm-2 control-label" for="input-name"><?php echo
$entry_name; ?></label>
    <div class="col-sm-10">
    <input type="text" name="name" value="<?php echo $name; ?>"
placeholder="<?php echo $entry_name; ?>" id="input-name" class="form-
control" />
      <?php if ($error_name) { ?>
      <div class="text-danger"><?php echo $error_name; ?></div>
    <?php } ?>
  </div>
</div>
```

The following code is used to show the language flags and language names. When you click on the required language tab, it loads the respective language tab fields:

```
<?php foreach ($languages as $language) { ?>
<li><a href="#language<?php echo $language['language_id']; ?>" data-
toggle="tab"><img src="view/image/flags/<?php echo $language['image'];
?>" title="<?php echo $language['name']; ?>" /> <?php echo
$language['name']; ?></a></li>
<?php } ?>
```

The following code iterates for the languages and creates a tab pane as per the language ID so that the respective tabs open when you click on the required language:

```
<?php foreach ($languages as $language) { ?>
<div class="tab-pane" id="language<?php echo $language['language_id'];
?>">
```

The following code outputs `<label class="col-sm-2 control-label" for="input-title1">Heading Title</label>`. Heading title is given by the `$entry_title` variable. Likewise, it also outputs the input box as `<input type="text" name="module_description[1][title]" placeholder="Heading Title" id="input-heading1" value="Home Page Hello World Heading Title" class="form-control">`. The input box name is `module_description[1][title]`, where `[1]` is the language ID:

```
<div class="form-group">
  <label class="col-sm-2 control-label" for="input-title<?php echo
$language['language_id']; ?>"><?php echo $entry_title; ?></label>
  <div class="col-sm-10">
    <input type="text" name="module_description[<?php echo
$language['language_id']; ?>][title]" placeholder="<?php echo $entry_
title; ?>" id="input-heading<?php echo $language['language_id']; ?>"
value="<?php echo isset($module_description[$language['language_id']]
['title']) ? $module_description[$language['language_id']]['title'] :
''; ?>" class="form-control" />
  </div>
</div>
```

The following code outputs the description text, which is given by the `$entry_description` variable. Likewise, it also outputs the text area box as `<textarea name="module_description[1][description]" placeholder="Description" id="input-description1" class="form-control" style="display: none;">&lt;p&gt;This is Home Page Hello World description field data&lt;/p&gt;</textarea>`.

The text area name is `module_description[1][description]`, where `[1]` is the language ID. It also has `id="input-description1"`, which is used for the WYSISYG HTML editor, and we know that OpenCart uses a third-party app called Summernote for the WYSISYG HTML editor:

```
<div class="form-group">
  <label class="col-sm-2 control-label" for="input-description<?php
echo $language['language_id']; ?>"><?php echo $entry_description; ?></
label>
  <div class="col-sm-10">
    <textarea name="module_description[<?php echo $language['language_
id']; ?>][description]" placeholder="<?php echo $entry_description;
?>" id="input-description<?php echo $language['language_
id']; ?>" class="form-control"><?php echo isset($module_
description[$language['language_id']]['description']) ? $module_
description[$language['language_id']]['description'] : ''; ?></
textarea>
```

```
    </div>
  </div>
</div>
<?php } ?>
```

The following code shows the `select` box for the status, which holds the enabled and disabled options:

```
<select name="status" id="input-status" class="form-control">
  <?php if ($status) { ?>
  <option value="1" selected="selected"><?php echo $text_enabled; ?></option>
  <option value="0"><?php echo $text_disabled; ?></option>
  <?php } else { ?>
  <option value="1"><?php echo $text_enabled; ?></option>
  <option value="0" selected="selected"><?php echo $text_disabled; ?></option>
  <?php } ?>
</select>
```

OpenCart 2 uses Summernote, the super-simple WYSIWYG editor on Bootstrap. You can get more details on the Summernote editor at http://summernote.org/:

```
<script type="text/javascript"><!--
  <?php foreach ($languages as $language) { ?>
$('#input-description<?php echo $language['language_id']; ?>').
summernote({height: 300});
  <?php } ?>
//--></script>
```

This code is meant for tabs when there is more than one language:

```
<script type="text/javascript"><!--
$('#language a:first').tab('show');
//--></script>
```

Creating a language file for the Catalog (frontend) module in OpenCart

There is no need to create the language file for our `Hello World` module, but in most cases a language file is needed. We can create a language file just as we created it in the admin section. For the frontend, your language file will be located in `catalog/language/english/module/MODULENAME.php`. The filename should be the same as the module name. As per the `Account` module, the language file's name is `account.php`, and the file is created at `catalog/language/english/account`. It consists of just the following code:

```
<?php
// Heading
$_['heading_title']     = 'Account';
```

The `Account` text is assigned to `heading_title`, and with the same `heading_title` it is accessible to the controller. The controller passes it to the view.

Creating a controller file for the Catalog (frontend) module in OpenCart

The controller file of the module for the frontend can be found in `catalog/controller/module/MODULENAME.php`. As per the `Hello World` module, we can see the `helloworld.php` file at `catalog/controller/module`. Since we named the file `helloworld.php` and put it into the `module` folder, the controller class name will be `ControllerModuleHelloworld`:

```
class ControllerModuleHelloworld extends Controller {
```

Also, always make sure your controller extends the parent controller class so that it can inherit all its functions:

```
public function index() {
```

If the second segment of the URI is empty, the `index()` function is always loaded by default. We can load the module controller as `http://example.com/index.php?route=module/helloworld/index` or `http://example.com/index.php?route=module/helloworld`.

Here, the second segment of the URI is `index`. If you have created some other function, then you can call the function of the module by passing it in the second segment of the URI:

```
$this->language->load('module/account');
```

A language file is loaded using the preceding line of code. In accordance with this line, the account.php file at catalog/language/english/account is loaded if the English language is active. Otherwise, it will load a file as per the language activated. For example if Spanish is active, then it loads the language file from catalog/language/spanish/module/:

```
$data['heading_title'] = $this->language->get('heading_title');
```

This line fetches the Account text with $this->language->get('heading_title');, and assigns it to the heading_title variable of the data array. The $heading_title variable will show as Account in the template files. In this way, we can add multiple-language support to our theme.

Our Hello World module controller's code is as follows:

```
public function index($setting) {
if (isset($setting['module_description'][$this->config->get('config_
language_id')])) {
$data['heading_title'] = html_entity_decode($setting['module_
description'][$this->config->get('config_language_id')]['title'], ENT_
QUOTES, 'UTF-8');
$data['helloworld'] = html_entity_decode($setting['module_
description'][$this->config->get('config_language_id')]
['description'], ENT_QUOTES, 'UTF-8');

if (file_exists(DIR_TEMPLATE . $this->config->get('config_template') .
'/template/module/helloworld.tpl')) {
return $this->load->view($this->config->get('config_template') . '/
template/module/helloworld.tpl', $data);
    } else {
return $this->load->view('default/template/module/helloworld.tpl',
$data);
    }
  }
}
```

The $setting variable holds all the details of the Hello World module. It holds its name and module description. The module_description array holds the title, description, and status.

The first line of code checks whether the description is inserted into the Hello World module for the activated language, or not. We can find the active language using $this->config->get('config_language_id').

You will be able to get the values of the setting table in the database by passing the key. For instance, if the setting table of the database consists of the row shown in the following screenshot:

setting_id	store_id	code	key	value	serialized
505	0	config	config_name	Your Store	0

If you want to show Your Store, then you can easily put it wherever you like in the controller, model, or template files. You just have to type this:

```
echo $this->config->get('config_name');
```

But if serialized is equal to 1, it means that the value is stored in a serialized array:

```
if (file_exists(DIR_TEMPLATE . $this->config->get('config_template') .
'/template/module/helloworld.tpl')) {
return $this->load->view($this->config->get('config_template') . '/
template/module/helloworld.tpl', $data);
} else {
return $this->load->view('default/template/module/helloworld.tpl',
$data);
}
```

You can get the active template name using $this->config->get('config_template');. The preceding lines of code check whether helloworld.tpl is in the active template or not. If the file is in the active template, then it used. Otherwise, it will use the default template. So, it is better if we keep the module's files in the default theme, because in future if we wish to change the template then the activated module for the old template may show errors.

Creating a template file for the Catalog (frontend) module in OpenCart

You can find the template file at catalog/view/theme/<template name>/module. As for the Hello World module, the filename is helloworld.tpl. OpenCart's frontend template files have a deeper folder structure than the admin folder structure because the admin section can have only one template. For frontend, there can be any number of templates, and among them one is selected by going to **Administrator | System | Settings | Edit** the store, and on the **Store** tab choose the most appropriate template in the **Template** field.

A folder named `<template name>` is created at `catalog/view/theme`. One of the basic rules in OpenCart is *never* to edit the default theme template file, because if OpenCart does not find a certain template file in your theme's `<template name>` folder then it will find it in the default theme. Also, while upgrading, the changes made on your custom theme will get overridden. If OpenCart does not find it even in the default theme, then it shows the following error:

```
Notice: Error: Could not load template catalog/view/theme/customtheme/
template/module/helloworld.tpl! in system\engine\controller.php
```

Here the theme folder's name is `customtheme`.

If you see this kind of error, it means that `helloworld.tpl` is missing from `customtheme` and from the default theme folder. So, you need to create the `helloworld.tpl` file in `catalog/view/theme/customtheme/template/module` or `catalog/view/theme/default/template/module`. Since `helloworld.tpl` is not a default file of OpenCart, we can place it in either `customtheme` or the default theme folder, but it is much better to place third-party modules in the default theme. Otherwise, if the website admin decides to switch themes later, then the module's file will be missed in the newly activated theme.

If you require any changes in the default theme's template files, then you have to copy the files and folder to the `customtheme` folder, and make the changes to the `customtheme` folder's files. This should be done so that, while upgrading, it will help preserve your changes. The following is the code in `catalog/view/theme/default/module/helloworld.tpl`:

```
<div>
  <h2><?php echo $heading_title; ?></h2>
  <?php echo $html; ?>
</div>
```

The `$heading_title` variable holds the `Hello World` text, and `$html` holds the message or text that is inserted into the `Hello World` module from the backend.

Summary

In this chapter, we cloned the HTML content module into the `Hello World` module. The `Hello World` module was created, installed, configured, and uninstalled. After configuration, we inserted some data and showed it at the frontend.

You found out how code works in the Hello World module and saw its file and folder structure. We described the code that we used in the Hello World module's files. By referring to the Hello World module, you should be able to go through other modules and become familiar with them. Now, we need to go deeper into the module, so in the next chapter we will describe the code for extensions. You will learn about the global library methods of OpenCart and how to create a shipping extension.

5
Extensions Code

In this chapter, we will see most of the code that is used in OpenCart to perform different functions, and it will be helpful in creating modules. We have used OpenCart version 2.0.1.1. You will learn the following topics in this chapter:

- Global library methods
- Detailed description of the Featured module
- Shipping and payment extensions
- Order Total extension

Global library methods

OpenCart has many predefined methods that can be called anywhere, for example, in controller, model, as well as view template files. You can find system-level library files at `system/library/`. We will show you how methods can be written and what their functions are.

Affiliate (affiliate.php)

You can find most of the affiliate code written in the affiliate section. You can check out the files at `catalog/controller/affiliate/` and `catalog/model/affiliate/`. Here is a list of methods we can use for the affiliate library:

- When an e-mail and password are passed to this method, it logs in to the affiliate section if the username (e-mail) and password match among the affiliates. You can find this code at `catalog/controller/affiliate/login.php` on validate method:

    ```
    $this->affiliate->login($email, $password);
    ```

- The affiliate gets logged out. This means the affiliate ID is cleared and its session is destroyed. Also, the affiliate's first name, last name, e-mail, telephone, and fax are given an empty value:

```
$this->affiliate->logout();
```

- Check whether the affiliate is logged in. If you like to show a message to the logged-in affiliate only, then you can use this code:

```
$this->affiliate->isLogged();
```

When we echo the following line, it will show the ID of the active affiliate:

```
if ($this->affiliate->isLogged()){
  echo "Welcome to the Affiliate Section";
} else {
  echo "You  are not at Affiliate Section";
}

$this->affiliate->getId();
```

- When we echo the following line, it will show the first name of the active affiliate:

```
$this->affiliate->getFirstName();
```

- When we echo the following line, it will show last name of the the active affiliate.

```
$this->affiliate->getLastName();
```

- When we echo the following line, it will show the active affiliate's e-mail:

```
$this->affiliate->getEmail();
```

- When we echo the following line, it will show telephone number of the the active affiliate:

```
$this->affiliate->getTelephone();
```

- When we echo the following line, it will show the fax number for the active affiliate:

```
$this->affiliate->getFax();
```

- When we echo the preceding line, it will show the active affiliate's tracking code, which is used to track referrals:

```
$this->affiliate->getCode();
```

Cache (cache.php)

The code written in the cache section can be found as follows:

- You can get the cache as per the key value passed with the following method:

```
$this->cache->get($key);
```

- In the following example, if it finds the cache of the country at the system/cache folder, it directly takes the data from there, as it has to perform the database query to retrieve the country:

```
$country_data = $this->cache->get('country');
if (!$country_data) {
$query = $this->db->query("SELECT * FROM " . DB_PREFIX ."country
ORDER BY name ASC");
$country_data = $query->rows;
$this->cache->set('country', $country_data);
}
return $country_data;

$this->cache->set($key, $value);
```

- It helps create the cache files. In the preceding example—regarding the country—if the cache file is not obtained, then the query to the database is performed and the retrieved data is set with the key of country:

```
$this->cache->delete($key);
```

It deletes the file in the cache folder as per the key provided. Like `$this->cache->delete('country');`. It deletes the cache file of the country that is at system/cache/.

Cart (cart.php)

The following system-instantiated cart objects are available for use:

- To get the list of all the products in the array of the cart, use the preceding code:

```
$this->cart->getProducts();
```

- To add a product to the cart, you just need to pass the product ID, which is compulsory, and your desired quantity. Your desired options and recurring ID are optional. If the quantity is not passed, the option will be null array and no recurring will be activated. The $recurring_id=0 sets the billing type the user has selected for that product, and the recurrence of products can be set by admin:

```
$this->cart->getRecurringProducts();
$this->cart->add($product_id, $qty = 1, $option =
array(),$recurring_id = 0);
```

- If you need to update the product in the cart, then the preceding method can be used, where $key is the product ID and $qty is the quantity you added:

```
$this->cart->update($key, $qty);
```

- If you want to remove the product from the cart, then use the preceding method, where $key is an array of the product line data (options, product_id, and recurring_id), which is serialized, and then base64 is used. This is the key, and the quantity is stored as the value for the key:

```
$this->cart->remove($key);
```

- If you want to remove all the products at once, then use the following method:

```
$this->cart->clear();
```

- The following code gives the sum of the weights of all products in the cart that have shipping requirment:

```
$this->cart->getWeight();
```

- The following code gives the subtotal of all products that are in the cart before tax:

```
$this->cart->getSubTotal();
```

- The following code gives the array of total taxes applied in the cart:

```
$this->cart->getTaxes();
```

- The following code gives the total cost of all products in the cart after tax:

```
$this->cart->getTotal();
```

- The following code gives the total number of the products in the cart:

```
$this->cart->countProducts();
```

- The following code checks whether the cart has a product or not. It returns an integer value:

```
$this->cart->hasProduct();
```

- The following code checks for the stock of each product in the cart. If it has some stock, it returns true. Otherwise, it returns false (which means there is no stock):

```
$this->cart->hasStock();
```

- The following code checks whether a product requires shipping or not. It does this for each product in the cart. If any of the products in the cart have shipping, true is returned. Otherwise, false is returned:

```
$this->cart->hasShipping();
```

- This following code checks whether the product is downloadable or not. It does this for each product in the cart. If any of the products in the cart are downloadable, `true` is returned. Otherwise, `false` is returned:

```
$this->cart->hasDownload();
```

Config (config.php)

The code found in `config.php` is as follows:

- The following code is used to override the preset value:

```
$this->config->set($key, $value);
```

- It does not save the value in the database. For example, if you like to show the different store name than the setting value, then do the following: in the controller, add the following code. Normally, when we echo `$this->config->get('config_name');`, we get the store name, but with the set value, we will get the store name as `New Store Name`:

```
$this->config->set('config_name','New Store Name');
```

- The following line of code returns the set value as per the $key passed. If there is no key value, then it returns null. For example, wherever you echo `$this->config->get('config_name');`, you will get the store name:

```
$this->config->get($key);
```

- The following code checks whether $key already exists or not:

```
$this->config->has($key);
```

- This code loads the configuration file in the `system/config/` folder.

```
$this->config->load($filename);
```

Currency (currency.php)

The `currency.php` has the following code available for use:

- The following code sets or overrides the currency code to be used in the session, as well as sets the cookie for the currency:

```
$this->currency->set($currency);
```

- It formats a number to the currency passed, as follows:

```
$this->currency->format($number, $currency='', $value='', $format=true);
```

- For example, if you have the number 100 and the currency as USD, then it will be formatted as $100.00. Here, $number is the price value, $currency is the currency code, $value is the conversion rate between the currencies, and $format is used to format of the currencies. Consider this example code:

```
$this->currency->format(50000, 'USD',  1, false);
```

- It outputs 50000.00:

```
$this->currency->format(50000, USD, 1, true);
```

- This outputs $50,000.00.

- We can find the settings when we insert the currency **Administrator | System | Localization | Currencies**, the currency sign, the position to show the sign, the decimal points to show, and so on:

- If the currency is set from **Administrator | System | Localization | Currencies**, then the value passed is converted to another currency passed:

```
$this->currency->convert($value, $from, $to);
```

- If you need the ID of the currency, then you have to use the getId function, for example, $this->currency->getId('USD'). You will get the ID of USD, which is the code of the currency inserted:

```
$this->currency->getId($currency='');
```

  If no currency code is defined, then it returns zero.

- For some currencies, the symbol is to the left of the value, for example, the US dollar ($100). If the left symbol is set, then we can get the symbol with the use of the following method as echo $this->currency->getSymbolLeft('USD');:

```
$this->currency->getSymbolLeft($currency='');
```

- For some currencies, the symbol is on the right of the value, for example, the Swedish krona, (100krona). If the symbol is set to the right, then we can get it with the following method as echo $this->currency->getSymbolRight(SEK);:

```
$this->currency->getSymbolRight($currency='');
```

- While inserting the currency by navigating to **Administrator | System | Localization | Currencies | Insert Button**, there is a field called **Decimal Places**. The same setting is activated as per the activated currency. If we insert 2 in the input field and save it, then, after the decimal, two numbers are shown, like this: $100.00. You can get to know it using echo $this->currency->getDecimalPlace('USD');:

```
$this->currency->getDecimalPlace($currency='');
```

- The following code gives the code that you insert as the ISO code by going to **Administrator | System | Localization | Currencies | Insert Button**. The same code will be returned:

  ```
  $this->currency->getCode();
  ```

- The following code gives the value entered in the Value field while inserting the currency. It is taken as the exchange rate for the specified currency with respect to the default currency:

  ```
  $this->currency->getValue($currency = '');
  ```

- The following code checks whether the passed currency exists in the OpenCart currency list. If it finds the currency, then it returns true. Otherwise, false is returned:

  ```
  $this->currency->has($currency);
  ```

Customer (customer.php)

In customer.php, the following code can be used:

- Use the following code to log a customer in. It checks for the customer username and password if $override is passed as false; otherwise, only for the current logged in status and the e-mail is checked:

  ```
  $this->customer->login($email, $password, $override = false);
  ```

  If it finds the correct entry, then the cart entry and wish list entries are retrieved. Also, the customer ID, first name, last name, e-mail, telephone, fax, newsletter subscription status, customer group ID, and address ID are globally accessible by the customer. It also updates the customer's IP address from where they logged in.

- When the following code is called, it logs out the customer. First of all, it updates the cart and wish list field of the customer table in the database and destroys the customer ID's session. Then, it assigns a blank value to the customer object's data, such as customer ID, first name, last name, e-mail, telephone, fax, newsletter, customer group ID, and address ID:

  ```
  $this->customer->logout();
  ```

- The first line of the following code checks whether the customer is logged in or not. If they are logged in, it returns TRUE. Otherwise, it returns FALSE. For instance, consider this code:

  ```
  $this->customer->isLogged();

  if($this->customer->isLogged()){
    echo"You are at the logged customer section";
  ```

```
}else{
  echo"You have not logged in yet";
}
```

- This method will return the customer ID of the logged in customer:

  ```
  $this->customer->getId();
  ```

- The following line will return the active customer's first name:

  ```
  $this->customer->getFirstName();
  ```

- The following line will return the active customer's last name:

  ```
  $this->customer->getLastName();
  ```

- The following line will return the active customer's e-mail:

  ```
  $this->customer->getEmail();
  ```

- The following line will return the active customer's telephone number:

  ```
  $this->customer->getTelephone();
  ```

- The following line will return the active customer's fax number:

  ```
  $this->customer->getFax();
  ```

- The following line will return either 0 or 1. If 1 is shown, it means the customer is subscribed to the newsletter. If 0 is shown, it means the customer is not subscribed to the newsletter:

  ```
  $this->customer->getNewsletter();
  ```

- The following line will return the active customer's group ID:

  ```
  $this->customer->getGroupId();
  ```

- When we echo the following line, it shows the active customer's default address ID:

  ```
  $this->customer->getAddressId();
  ```

- When we echo the following line, it will show the active customer's current balance. When you click the Your Transaction link after logged in to the customer section, you will find the total current balance. The same balance is shown by the following code:

  ```
  $this->customer->getBalance();
  ```

- When we echo the following line, it will show the active customer's total remaining reward points.

  ```
  $this->customer->getRewardPoints();
  ```

Database (db.php)

MySQL is the default database and only supported database. Moreover, OpenCart does not come with SQL helper routines, so its models are full of MySQL's proprietary queries. This makes it really hard to port OpenCart to other database backends. We should not forget to add DB_PREFIX when referencing a table name. The reason for using database methods instead of standard MySQL/PHP functions, such as `last_insert_id`, `mysql_escape`, and so on, is that it separates the database engine types. If the user uses a different type of database driver, then no changes are needed in the code, as each database class will use the same method names, but will then map to the specific database type function name.

- The following code executes the passed SQL statement:

  ```
  $this->db->query($sql);
  ```

  Consider this example:

  ```
  $query = $this->db->query("SHOW COLUMNS FROM `".DB_
  PREFIX."product` LIKE 'youtube'");
  if (!$query->num_rows){
          $this->db->query("ALTER TABLE `".DB_PREFIX."product`
  ADD `youtube` TEXT NOT NULL");
  }
  ```

- When these lines of code are written in the controller or model files of OpenCart, it searches for the YouTube column in the product table, and if it does not find it, it alters the product table by adding another column named YouTube:

  ```
  $this->db->escape($value);
  ```

- This "escapes" or cleans the data before entering it in the database so that there is not extra SQL injection. You have to perform this for security reasons. If the value is an integer, then you can perform type casting the data type as `(int)$value`. If the data is a string, then use `$this->db->escape($value);`.

- The preceding code returns the count of affected rows by the most recent query execution:

  ```
  $this->db->countAffected($sql);
  ```

- This returns the ID of the last inserted rows by the most recent query execution.

  ```
  $this->db->getLastId($sql);
  ```

Document (document.php)

Document library methods can be called from the controller only before rendering the document:

- This line of code sets the page title:

```
$this->document->setTitle($title);
```

- The following line of code gets the page title:

```
$this->document->getTitle();
```

- This line of code sets the page's meta-description:

```
$this->document->setDescription($description);
```

- The following line of code gets the page's meta-description:

```
$this->document->getDescription();
```

- This line of code sets the page's meta tag keyword:

```
$this->document->setKeywords($keywords);
```

- The following line of code gets the page's meta tag keyword:

```
$this->document->getKeywords();
```

  For the **OpenCart** home page, title, and description, keywords are accessed from the settings inserted at Edit Store, which can be found by going to **System** | **Settings**. For other pages, the title and description are set as defined to override the default value as per the need of the controller:

```
$this->document->addLink($href, $rel);
```

- The following code adds the link in the head section as given:

```
$this->document->addLink($this->url->link('product/product',
'product_id=42','canonical'));
```

- If we write the following line of code in the controller, then we will see the following code in the head section:

```
<link href="http://example.com/index.php?route=product/
product&amp;product_id=42" rel="canonical" />
```

A canonical page is a page that you specify for the search engine, the preferred version among many pages with the same content. For example, one page might display products sorted in alphabetical order, and another page might show the same products sorted by the product model. A third page might display the same products listed by price, by rating, in multiple categories, or at the URL structure when SEO URLs are enabled included the category slug as well. You might end up with many URLs with the same product page content, so it is best to use the canonical rel:

- The details of canonical page are at `http://support.google.com/webmasters/bin/answer.py?hl=en&answer=139394`.

- The following code lists the link set. Mostly, calls are made in the header controller:

```
$this->document->getLinks();
```

- The following code adds the extra style sheet needed in the page only. Here's an example of its use:

```
$this->document->addStyle($href, $rel = 'stylesheet', $media = 'screen');
```

  The `colorbox.css` is needed in the product details page, so it is called in `catalog/controller/product/product.php` and the style sheet is added to the `head` section of the document:

```
$this->document->addStyle('catalog/view/javascript/jquery/colorbox/colorbox.css');
```

- The following code lists the style sheet in the `head` section of the document. Mostly, calls are made at the header controller:

```
$this->document->getStyles();
```

  As with `addStyle`, `colorbox.css` is added, so a line is added in the `head` section of the document. The following is the line we see in the `head` section of the document:

```
<link rel="stylesheet" type="text/css" href="catalog/view/javascript/jquery/colorbox/colorbox.css" media="screen" />
```

- The following code adds the script files needed in the page only, such as JavaScript files. This is an example of its use:

```
$this->document->addScript($script);
```

- This adds the `tabs.js` files wherever the preceding line of code is added. However, it is not always best practice to use this to add scripts. Many scripts should be added at the end of a page load to improve performance. Mostly, we can use the view section to add extra JavaScript:

```
$this->document->addScript('catalog/view/javascript/jquery/tabs.
js');
```

- The following code lists the script files added by addScript:

```
$this->document->getScripts();
```

With the `addScript` code, as shown in the preceding example, `tabs.js` file is added, so a line is added in the `head` section of the document. This line of code is added:

```
<script type="text/javascript"src="catalog/view/javascript/jquery/
tabs.js"></script>
```

Encryption (encryption.php)

The following methods can be used from `encryption.php`:

- The following code encrypts data based on the key in the admin settings:

```
$this->encryption->encrypt($value);
```

- This code decrypts data based on the key in the admin settings:

```
$this->encryption->decrypt($value);
```

Language (language.php)

The following methods can be used from `language.php`:

- The following code gets the value of the key from the language file. Here's an example of its use:

```
$this->language->get($key);
```

- The following code searches for the value of `heading_title` in the language file:

```
$this->language->get('heading_title');
```

- The following code loads the language file and made its variable for use:

```
$this->language->load($filename);
```

- This loads `catalog/language/english/catalog/category.php` when the English language is active, or loads the respective language's `category.php`.

```
$this->language->load('catalog/category');
```

Length (length.php)

In `length.php`, the following methods can be used:

- The passed value is converted as per the value provided:

```
$this->length->convert($value, $from, $to);
```

The configured length is converted to UPS length:

```
$length = $this->length->convert($this->config->get('ups_length'),
$this->config->get('config_length_class_id'), $this->config-
>get('ups_length_class_id'));
```

- The value passed is formatted to the required length format.

```
$this->length->format($value, $length_class_id, $decimal_point =
'.', $thousand_point = ',');
```

- This code returns the length's unit such as centimeters, inches, and so on.

```
$this->length->getUnit($length_class_id);
```

Log (log.php)

To write a message passed to the `system | logs | error.txt` file, use the following code:

```
$this->log->write($message);
```

- Here is its example:

```
$this->log->write('This is the error message');
```

- If you write this line and reload the URL that calls this file, then the **This is the error message** message is logged in the `error.txt` file. You can also create your own log files for your modules simply by creating a new instance of this class, like this, for example:

```
$my_log=new Log('my_log_file.txt');
$my_log->write("This is my message");
```

Mail (mail.php)

You are shown an example directly for a mail, which will help you understand this more clearly.

- With these lines of code, an e-mail is sent.

```
$mail = new Mail();
$mail->setTo($this->request->post['email']);
    $mail->setFrom($this->config->get('config_email'));
    $mail->setSender($this->config->get('config_name'));
$mail->setSubject(html_entity_decode($subject, ENT_QUOTES, 'UTF-
8'));
$mail->setText(html_entity_decode($message, ENT_QUOTES, 'UTF-8'));
    $mail->send();
```

- The setTo function sets for whom to send the mail
- The setFrom function sets by which the mail is sent
- The setSender sets the name of the sender
- The setSubject sets the subject section of the mail
- The setText is set for the message is it only text (if it is an HTML e-mail, then we use setHtml
- The send function sends the mail

Pagination (pagination.php)

The following variables are used in the code snippets, are parts of the user's listing:

- $user_total is the total number of the users
- $page is the page number that is available through the GET value
- limit is set by the admin
- text shows the page numbers and extra messages
- url is used to move to another page

Let's have a look at the code snippet:

```
$pagination = new Pagination();
$pagination->total = $user_total;
$pagination->page = $page;
$pagination->limit = $this->config->get('config_admin_limit');
```

```
$pagination->text = $this->language->get('text_pagination');
$pagination->url = $this->url->link('user/user', 'token=' . $this-
>session->data['token'] . $url .'&page={page}', 'SSL');
   $this->data['pagination'] = $pagination->render();
```

With this rendering, `$pagination` is available for the template view for showing the page numbers.

Request (request.php)

Two commonly used methods for a request-response between a client and server are GET and POST:

- In OpenCart, these are written as:
  ```
  $this->request->get
  $this->request->post
  ```

- For the `'selected'` element, it is written as:
  - GET: `$this->request->get['selected']`
  - POST: `$this->request->post['selected']`

We can sanitize the data using `$this->clean($value);`. All the methods from request are as follows, and they are used for each form method passed:

```
$this->get = $this->clean($_GET);
$this->post = $this->clean($_POST);
$this->request = $this->clean($_REQUEST);
$this->cookie = $this->clean($_COOKIE);
$this->files = $this->clean($_FILES);
$this->server = $this->clean($_SERVER);
```

Developers should never use the `$_GET` or `$_POST` variables unless they know how to sanitize the data.

Response (response.php)

In `response.php`, the following methods can be used

- The `addHeader` method adds the content type used by the document. A JSON content type header should be added before any JSON data is returned, which is usually used by AJAX calls using controllers.
  ```
  $response = new Response();
  $response->addHeader('Content-Type: text/html; charset=utf-8');
  ```

- This code redirects the page to the specified URL. The $url passed should be a complete URL. For example, when you insert the category and click on the save button, then you are redirected to the category listing page.

```
$this->redirect($url);
```

Session (session.php)

The following methods can be used in session.php:

- To return the active session ID, use this code:

```
$this->session->getId();
```

- To destroy all active sessions, we use the following code:

```
$this->session->destroy();
```

Tax (tax.php)

In tax.php, the following methods can be used:

- The following code sets the shipping address with the country ID and zone ID:

```
$this->tax->setShippingAddress($country_id, $zone_id);
```

- The following code sets the payment address with the country ID and zone ID:

```
$this->tax->setPaymentAddress($country_id, $zone_id);
```

- The following code sets the store address with the country ID and zone ID:

```
$this->tax->setStoreAddress($country_id, $zone_id);
```

- The following code calculates the tax only if tax_class_id is set and calculate is set as true:

```
$this->tax->calculate($value, $tax_class_id, $calculate = true);
```

URL (url.php)

The following methods can be used in url.php:

- This code makes the URL with as passed of the route. If $secure is true, then SSL is active, and it makes https URL non-SSL, which makes the URL http:

```
$this->url->link($route, $args = '', $secure = false)
```

User (user.php)

In user.php, the following list of methods can be used:

- When we echo the preceding line, it will show the active user's ID:

  ```
  $this->user->getId();
  ```

- When the username and password are passed to the method, it logs in to the administration section if the username and password match among the users:

  ```
  $this->user->login($username, $password);
  ```

- The admin user gets logged out. This means that the user ID is cleared and its session is destroyed. Also, the username and user ID are assigned empty values:

  ```
  $this->user->logout();
  ```

- The following code checks whether the user is logged in or not. It actually returns the ID of the user who is logged in:

  ```
  $this->user->isLogged();
  ```

- The following code checks whether the user has permission or not. This is an example of its use:

  ```
  $this->user->hasPermission($key, $value)
  ```

- The following code checks whether the user is provided with access to modify or insert categories. Permission for users can be provided from **User Group**, which is found by going to **Administrator | System | Users**. Edit or insert the user given the necessary permission to the user:

  ```
  if (!$this->user->hasPermission('modify', 'catalog/category)) {
          $this->error['warning'] = $this->language->get('error_
  permission');
      }
  ```

- The following code returns the active user ID:

  ```
  $this->user->getId();
  ```

- This code returns the active user's username:

  ```
  $this->user->getUserName();
  ```

Weight (weight.php)

The following code can be used in `weight.php`:

- The passed value is converted as per the value provided to the desired weight. The `$value` is the weight of products in the shopping cart, and `$from` is the variable from the `weight` class needed to convert to the `$to` variable from the `weight` class. You can insert and edit the weight class by going to **Administrator | System | Weight Class**:

  ```
  $this->weight->convert($value, $from, $to);
  ```

- The value passed is formatted to required weight format:

  ```
  $this->weight->format($value, $weight_class_id, $decimal_point =
  '.', $thousand_point = ',');
  ```

- This code returns the weight's unit, such as kilogram, pound, gram, and so on:

  ```
  $this->length->getUnit($weight_class_id);
  ```

The Featured module

The Featured module highlights specific products so that it will be helpful in increasing sales and lets others know which products are highlighted.

Configuring the Featured module in OpenCart 2.0.1.1

The following steps help configure the Featured module:

1. Log in to the **Administrator** dashboard. Hover over **Extensions**, and then click on **Modules**. You will see a list of modules.

2. If the **Featured** module is not already installed, then click on the green install button, or you can start by clicking on the blue edit button in order to configure the featured product. Upon clicking on the blue edit button of the Featured product, the following screen is seen:

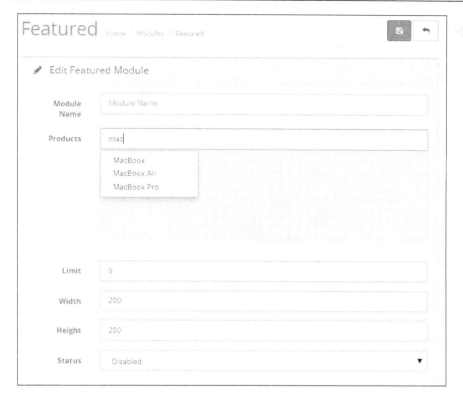

3. Enter the module name, which will be shown in the **Layout** section.

4. Now, start typing the name of the product in the **Products** field. It will autocomplete and pop up a list of the names of products that match with the words of the typed product name. Choose the product you want to show in the featured products and it will be shown in the list. Now, to add another product, just start typing again and choose the right product. Like this, you can make a list of featured products. If you don't want a product on the featured list, then click on the black minus sign to the left of the product, and the product will be removed from the list:

    ○ **Limit**: This is the number of products to be shown. Although we insert many products, only a limited number of products are shown.

    ○ **Width**: Insert the width for the product's image, which is in pixels.

    ○ **Height**: Insert the height for the product's image, which is in pixels.

    ○ **Status**: Shows at the frontend only if it is enabled.

5. After these are set, go to the Layout section and insert the Featured module into the required layout.

Exploring code used in Featured module

When you click on the `[Edit]` of the installed Featured module, the `module/featured` route is called. It means that there is a file named `featured.php` in the module folder on controller. So, let's start listing the files used by the Featured module:

- `admin/controller/module/featured.php`
- `admin/language/english/module/featured.php`
- `admin/view/template/module/featured.tpl`
- `catalog/controller/module/featured.php`
- `catalog/language/english/module/featured.php`
- `catalog/view/theme/default/template/module/featured.tpl`

Exploring the code of admin/controller/module/featured.php

The OpenCart controller is just a class file that is named in a way that can be associated with a URI. The class name should start with the word `Controller`, then contain the folder name, and finally contain the filename, like this for example:

```
classControllerModuleFeatured extends Controller {
```

Here, the `Controller` class is the name of the Featured module. The class name starts with Controller, along with the module folder. Then, the featured file, as the featured module controller file, is named `featured.php` and is in the module folder and extended to the parent Controller.

If the filename consists of an underscore (_), then there will be no problem with corresponding to the class name. Excluding the underscore, the other needs to be the same. If the controller file has an underscore in the filename, the language file should have an underscore as well. Never use an underscore for a class name.

Most of the related code is already described in the description of the Hello World module, so we are describing only the functionality.

By default, the index method is called, unless the third segment is passed in the URI. By clicking on **Edit**, no second segment is passed, so it runs the index function called `public function index() {`. It loads the language files named `featured.php` in the module folder in the language section. This sets the title of document with `$this->document->setTitle($this->language->get('heading_title'));`. Then it loads the `setting.php` model, and when the module is saved, it validates the data by checking the permission and checking whether the image size is inserted or not, check the `protected function validate()` and you find out how it returns TRUE when validation is successful, assigns the error message, and returns false if there is some error, for example, if permission is denied or the image's height and width are not entered:

```
if (isset($this->request->post['featured_module'])) {
foreach ($this->request->post['featured_module'] as $key => $value) {
  if (!$value['image_width'] || !$value['image_height']) {
    $this->error['image'][$key] = $this->language->get('error_image');
  }
}
}
```

The preceding code shows how an error message gets activated if the height and width are not entered on saving the module:

```
$data['heading_title'] = $this->language->get('heading_title');
$data['text_edit'] = $this->language->get('text_edit');
$data['text_enabled'] = $this->language->get('text_enabled');
$data['text_disabled'] = $this->language->get('text_disabled');
```

Text and messages to be shown in the view are assigned from language files to data variables. You can see similar lines of code that perform this:

```
if (isset($this->error['width'])) {
$data['error_width'] = $this->error['width'];
} else {
  $data['error_width'] = '';
}
if (isset($this->error['height'])) {
  $data['error_height'] = $this->error['height'];
} else {
  $data['error_height'] = '';
}
```

If someone forgets to insert the height and width, then the error messages to be shown are assigned.

Breadcrumbs are defined in the `$data['breadcrumbs']` array, and the required links are defined like this:

```
$data['action'] = $this->url->link('module/featured', 'token=' .
$this->session->data['token'], 'SSL');
```

The list of products that you have inserted is submitted with the `$_POST` method, and each product's ID is separated by a comma. Products stored in the database for Featured modules are also saved as product IDs separated by commas in a serialized array. You can view the `oc_module` table through **PhpMyAdmin**, as shown in the following screenshot:

The following lines of code check whether the featured product module is submitted and perform the validation. They also check the following: whether the user has permission to modify it, whether the module name is inserted, and whether the height and width of the image are inserted. After validation, it checks whether `module_id` is set. If it is not set, then the module is added nor does it edit the feature module:

```
if (($this->request->server['REQUEST_METHOD'] == 'POST') && $this-
>validate()) {
  if (!isset($this->request->get['module_id'])) {
$this->model_extension_module->addModule('featured', $this->request-
>post);
  } else {
$this->model_extension_module->editModule(
$this->request->get['module_id'], $this->request->post);
  }
```

```
    $this->session->data['success'] =
$this->language->get('text_success');
$this->response->redirect($this->url->link('extension/module',
'token=' . $this->session->data['token'], 'SSL'));
}
```

The next code is used to set the value for the module name. If the form is submitted and has some errors, then it sets the recently submitted value using `$data['name'] = $this->request->post['name'];`. Likewise, if you are editing a module, and the `module_info` is not empty, then it sets the value as `$data['name'] = $module_info['name'];`. Otherwise, it sets an empty value:

```
if (isset($this->request->post['name'])) {
    $data['name'] = $this->request->post['name'];
} elseif (!empty($module_info)) {
    $data['name'] = $module_info['name'];
} else {
    $data['name'] = '';
}
```

Similarly, it sets such values for `$data['products']`, `$data['limit']`, `$data['width']`, and `$data['status']`:

```
$data['header'] = $this->load->controller('common/header');
$data['column_left'] = $this->load->controller('common/column_left');
$data['footer'] = $this->load->controller('common/footer');
$this->response->setOutput($this->load->view('module/featured.tpl',
$data));
```

This code is used to load the header, `column_left`, and footer for the Featured module. In the template section, we can perform `<?php echo $header; ?>` to show the header section. The `$this->response->setOutput()` line sends the data to the browser whether it's HTML or JSON (which needs a JSON header type), and `$data` sends all of the data as a variable that is accessible from the template page.

Exploring the code of admin/view/template/module/featured.tpl

In this section, we are describing only the extra code, as most of this code has already been described in the Hello World module.

The most distinguishing section in Featured module is the autocomplete input box:

```
<input type="text" name="product" value="" placeholder="<?php echo
$entry_product; ?>" id="input-product" class="form-control" />
```

It shows the input field for entering the product name. When we choose the products, those products are shown in the `id="featured-product"` div:

```
<div id="featured-product" class="well well-sm" style="height: 150px;
overflow: auto;">
    <?php foreach ($products as $product) { ?>
<div id="featured-product<?php echo $product['product_id']; ?>"><i
class="fa fa-minus-circle"></i> <?php echo $product['name']; ?>
<input type="hidden" name="product[]" value="<?php echo
$product['product_id']; ?>" />
        </div>
    <?php } ?>
</div>
```

Whenever users start typing, the `$('input[name=\'product\']').` `autocomplete({})` code starts working. It searches for similarly named products in `admin/index.php?route=catalog/product/autocomplete`. If it finds the products, then on clicking the product, it gets appended to the featured-product ID's div and makes a product list like the following code, which is shown near the bottom of `admin/view/template/module/featured.tpl`:

```
$('#featured-product').append('<div id="featured-product' +
item['value'] + '"><i class="fa fa-minus-circle"></i> ' +
item['label'] + '<input type="hidden" name="product[]" value="' +
item['value'] + '" /></div>');
```

When you click on the red minus sign just to the right of the product, the following code is activated. It deletes the rows of the product:

```
$('#featured-product').delegate('.fa-minus-circle', 'click',
function() {
    $(this).parent().remove();
});
```

Exploring the code of catalog/controller/module/featured.php

Only the extra code is described in this section, as most of it has been discussed in *Chapter 1, Getting Started with OpenCart 2.0*, and most of its parts are similar to the Hello World module:

```
if (!$setting['limit']) {
    $setting['limit'] = 4;
}
```

If there is no limit inserted while setting the Featured module, then it will show only five products. If we write the following code in the module's controller, then it shows an array that has the keys and values of the module:

```
echo "<pre>";
print_r($setting);
```

If you write the preceding code in `catalog/controller/module/featured.php` and reload it where the Featured module is activated, then you will see something like this:

```
Array
(
        [name] => Featured Products
        [product] => Array
            (
                [0] => 43
                [1] => 40
                [2] => 42
                [3] => 30
            )

        [limit] => 4
        [width] => 200
        [height] => 200
        [status] => 1
)
```

```
$products = array_slice($setting['product'], 0,
(int)$setting['limit']);
```

This code extracts the products of the `slice` array. The same is used to retrieve the products of the featured product module. An iteration is done with `foreach` on the $products array. With the help of `$this->model_catalog_product->getProduct($product_id)`;, all the details of the product are retrieved, and only the required elements are assigned to the products array to be passed to the template file:

```
$data['products'][] = array(
    'product_id'  => $product_info['product_id'],
    'thumb'       => $image,
    'name'        => $product_info['name'],
    'description' => utf8_substr(strip_tags(html_entity_decode($product_
    info['description'], ENT_QUOTES, 'UTF-8')), 0, $this->config-
    >get('config_product_description_length')) . '..',
    'price'       => $price,
    'special'     => $special,
```

```
    'tax'          => $tax,
    'rating'       => $rating,
  'href'           => $this->url->link('product/product', 'product_id=' .
  $product_info['product_id'])
  );
```

With the preceding code, only the required data, such as `product_id`, `thumb`, `name`, and so on, is assigned to the array, which will be shown in the template file.

The code of `catalog/view/theme/default/template/module/featured.tpl` is similar to the Hello World module's front template file. Here, the products that are added to the backend are shown. The `$products` array is received from the controller, which consists of the product ID, the thumb of the image, name, price, special price, rating, reviews, and links to the product details. The same data is shown in the Featured module's frontend.

The Shipping module

OpenCart has many prebuilt shipping modules. Go to **Administrator | Extension | Shipping**. You will see a list of shipping modules, as shown in the following screenshot:

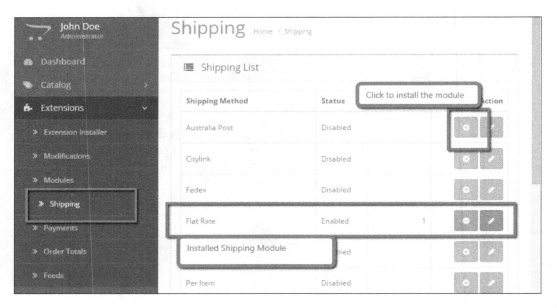

You have to install and configure the module, and it will be shown at the frontend under **Shipping Method** while performing a checkout.

As you already know, modules or extensions can be created by cloning any existing one that does something similar to what you want. So, for shipping, we will be cloning any one of them that fulfils our requirement.

For example, if you want the shipping cost to be charged as per the total cost purchased, then you can make a clone of the weight-based shipping module. Likewise, if you want to create a DHL shipping rates module using live rate lookup from the DHL site, you need to start with the existing UPS shipping extension. Let's start creating the shipping module that is based on the total cost purchased.

Changes required at the admin folder to create total cost based Shipping module

The following steps need to be carried out for creating the total cost based Shipping module:

1. Go to `admin/controller/shipping/`, copy `weight.php`, paste it in the same folder, rename it to `totalcost.php`, and open it to your favorite text editor. Then, find the following lines:

   ```
   classControllerShippingWeight extends Controller {
   ```

   Change the class name to this:

   ```
   classControllerShippingTotalcost extends Controller {
   ```

   Now find `weight` and replace all its occurrences with `totalcost`. Then, save the file.

2. Go to `admin/language/english/shipping`, copy `weight.php`, and paste it in the same folder. Rename it to `totalcost.php` and open it. Then, find the following code:

   ```
   $_['help_rate']        = 'Example: 5:10.00,7:12.00
   Weight:Cost,Weight:Cost, etc..';
   ```

   Then, make the changes as shown here:

   ```
   $_['help_rate']        = 'Example: 25:10.00,50:12.00 Total
   Cost:Shipping Cost,Total Cost:Shipping Cost, etc..';
   ```

   Next, find `Weight` and replace all its occurrences with `Total Cost`.

3. Go to `admin/view/template/shipping`, copy `weight.tpl`, and paste it in the same folder. Rename it to `totalcost.tpl` and open it. Then, find `weight` and replace it with `totalcost`. Finally, save the file.

Changes made in the catalog folder

The following changes need to be made in the `catalog` folder:

1. Go to `catalog/model/shipping` and copy `weight.php`. Paste it in the same folder and rename it to `totalcost.php`. Open it and find the following line:

   ```
   classModelShippingWeight extends Model {
   ```

   Change the class name to this:

   ```
   classModelShippingTotalcost extends Model {
   ```

   Now, find `weight` and replace all its occurrences with `totalcost`.

   After performing the replacement, find the following lines of code:

   ```
   $totalcost = $this->cart->gettotalcost();
   ```

   Make the changes as shown here:

   ```
   $totalcost = $this->cart->getSubTotal();
   ```

   Our requirement is to show the shipping cost as per the total cost purchased, so we have made the change you just saw.

2. Now, find these lines of code:

   ```
   if ((string)$cost != '') {
   $quote_data['totalcost_' . $result['geo_zone_id']] = array(
   'code'=>'totalcost.totalcost_'.$result['geo_zone_id'],
   'title'=>$result['name'].'('.$this->language->get('text_
   totalcost') . ' ' . $this->totalcost->format($totalcost, $this-
   >config->get('config_totalcost_class_id')) . ')',
      'cost'            => $cost,
   'tax_class_id' => $this->config->get('totalcost_tax_class_id'),
   'text'=> $this->currency->format($this->tax->calculate($cost,
   $this->config->get('totalcost_tax_class_id'), $this->config-
   >get('config_tax')))
   );
   }
   ```

   In them, consider the following lines:

   ```
   'title'=>$result['name'].'('.$this->language->get('text_
   totalcost') . ' ' . $this->totalcost->format($totalcost, $this-
   >config->get('config_totalcost_class_id')) . ')',
   ```

   Make this change, as we only need the name:

   ```
   'title' => $result['name'],
   ```

Weight has different classes, such as `kilogram`, `gram`, `pound`, and so on, but in our total cost purchased, we did not have any class specified so we removed it.

3. Save the file.

4. Go to `catalog/language/english/shipping` and copy `weight.php`. Paste it in the same folder and rename it to `totalcost.php`. Open it, find `Weight`, and replace it with `Total Cost`.

With these changes, the module is ready to install. Go to **Admin | Extensions | Shipping**, and then find `Total Cost Based Shipping`. Click on **Install** and grant permission to modify and access to the user. Then, edit to configure it. In the **General** tab, change the status to **Enabled**.

Other tabs are loaded as per the geo zones setting.

The default geo zones for OpenCart are set as **UK Shipping** and **UK VAT**.

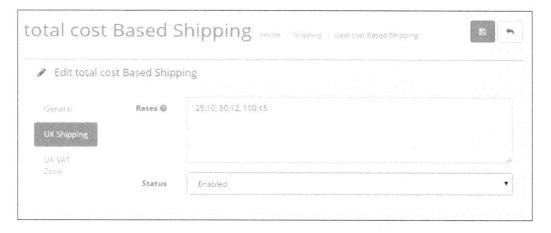

Now, insert the value for **Total Cost** versus **Rates**. If the subtotal reaches 25, then the shipping cost is 10; if it reaches 50, then the shipping cost is 12; and if it reaches 100, then the shipping cost is 15. So, we have inserted `25:10, 50:12, 100:15`. If the customer tries to order more than the inserted total cost, then no shipping is activated.

In this way, you can now clone the shipping modules and make changes to the logic as per your requirement.

The Payment module

Any module can be created by cloning an existing module with a similar functionality. By doing so, coding will become very easy and fast. You can view the list of Payment modules by going to **Administrator | Extensions | Payments**.

You can also create a payment module in a manner similar to that of the shipping module. To create a payment module, we have to work in the payment folder.

Before starting to write a payment module, you need to know about on-site payment and off-site payment, which are two broad categories of payment methods.

Off-site payment

Off-side payment means making a payment to the payment service by redirecting to a payment service website. The transaction is made at the payment service, and upon success or failure, the user is redirected to the relevant page. If the payment is successful, it shows a success message. Otherwise, it shows a failure message.

Some off-site payment modules are Paypal Standard, Moneybookers, LiqPay, and PayPoint.

If you are using off-site payment, then choose one of the off-side payment modules in OpenCart and clone it into your desired payment modules.

On-site payment

On-site means payments are made on the same site as the purchase. The customer doesn't leave your site to make the payment. Some on-site OpenCart payment modules are Authorize.net's AIM, Paypal Pro, and SagePay Direct.

When using on-site payment, it is recommended to have an SSL certificate, and SSL is enabled when setting OpenCart. All sites should use SSL, though it is optional, and SSL will improve user approval and user confidence.

If you are using on-site payment, choose one of the on-site payment modules and clone it to create your desired module. Most of the code will be the same; only the catalog controller file and some time view template forms need to be changed while creating the payment modules.

Order Total

Order total modules are those modules that affect the total price of the order. You can find a list of order totals by going to **Administrator | Extensions | Order Totals**. Some of them are as follows:

- **Coupon**: This allows the customer to apply a coupon discount
- **Store Credit**: If you have store credit, then it automatically decreases the total purchase cost with the available credits

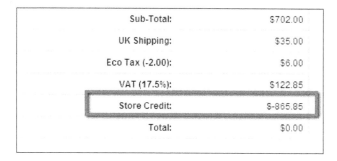

Sub-Total:	$702.00
UK Shipping:	$35.00
Eco Tax (-2.00):	$6.00
VAT (17.5%):	$122.85
Store Credit:	$-865.85
Total:	$0.00

- **Handling Fee**: This is the additional fee for handling the product
- **Low Order Fee**: This is the extra cost if the customer orders the minimum specified quantity or amount
- **Reward Points**: Points are accumulated, and they can be used to buy reward point products
- **Sub-total**: This shows the subtotal separately
- **Taxes**: This shows the taxes separately
- **Total**: This is the total amount to be billed
- **Gift Voucher**: The gift credit is used to purchase products

When handling fee, low-order fee, reward points, subtotal, taxes, total, and gift voucher are applied, there is a change on the order's total cost, so they are placed in the order total.

You will be able to see an order total module in the next chapter. We will show you how to create it. We will look at the Tips Order total module in depth. When someone adds Tips, there is an increase on the order total.

Summary

In this chapter, we explored most of the system-level libraries that OpenCart provides. Explore most of the extra code used in the featured product module, because of which you are now able to know the code flow of the OpenCart module. Likewise, we created a new shipping module that shows the shipping cost depending on the total cost purchased by cloning weight-based shipping. Similarly, we discussed the payment module of OpenCart and the ways to clone it. With this, you are now able to start coding with OpenCart extensions (Modules, Payment, and Shipping). In the next chapter, you will learn how to create custom pages and write the code required to perform the CRUD functionality.

6
Create OpenCart Custom Pages

In this chapter, we will create OpenCart custom pages in the admin and the frontend sections to show feedback, and describe how code is managed and how it works. You have already seen how to duplicate or clone a module in the previous chapters, while creating the `Hello World` and `Total Cost Shipping` modules, and likewise seen most of the global methods which will help you create modules.

In this chapter, you will learn the following topics:

- Creating feedback custom pages, so that admin will be able to write feedback about the site and show it on the frontend
- Creating feedback management pages
- Ways to create database tables for OpenCart
- Creating admin section pages to execute the CRUD functionality
- Creating presentations or viewing section pages to list feedback that is inserted by the admin

Getting started with feedback management

We will show you the way to create an admin form and a list page. After that, we will move on to create frontend pages where we display lists of feedback. Our feedback management will have author details, a feedback description, a status, and a date added. These will be shown in the frontend.

Database tables for feedback

Let's begin by creating tables in the database. We all know that OpenCart has multistore abilities, supports multiple languages, and can be displayed in multiple layouts, so when creating a database we should take this into consideration. Four tables are created: feedback, feedback_description, feedback_to_layout, and feedback_to_store. A feedback table is created for saving feedback-related data, and feedback_description is created for storing multiple-language data for the feedback. A feedback-to-layout table is created for saving the association of layout to feedback, and a feedback-to-store table is created for saving the association of store to feedback.

When we install OpenCart, we use oc_ as a **database prefix** as shown in the following image and query. A database prefix is defined in config.php where mostly you find something such as define('DB_PREFIX', 'oc_');, or what you entered when installing OpenCart. We create the oc_feedback table. It saves the status, sort order, date added, and feedback ID. Then we create the oc_feedback_ description table, where we will save the feedback writer's name, feedback given, and language ID, for multiple languages. Then we create the oc_feedback_to_ store table to save the store ID and feedback ID and keep the relationship between feedback and whichever store's feedback is to be shown. Finally, we create the oc_feedback_to_layout table to save the feedback_id and layout_id to show the feedback for the layout you want. This diagram shows the database schema:

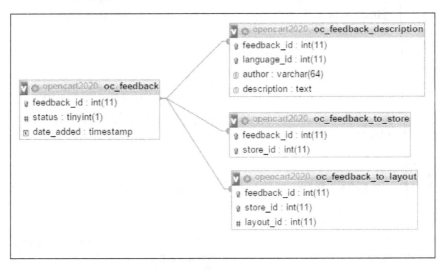

We need to run the following queries to create the feedback table, feedback_description table, feedback_to_layout table, and feedback_to_store table in the database.

If you have used a prefix other than oc_, then replace oc_ with your database prefix in these queries. Then you are ready to run these queries:

```
CREATE TABLE IF NOT EXISTS `oc_feedback` (
  `feedback_id` int(11) NOT NULL AUTO_INCREMENT,
  `status` tinyint(1) NOT NULL DEFAULT '0',
  `date_added` timestamp NOT NULL DEFAULT CURRENT_TIMESTAMP,
  PRIMARY KEY (`feedback_id`)
);

CREATE TABLE IF NOT EXISTS `oc_feedback_description` (
  `feedback_id` int(11) NOT NULL,
  `language_id` int(11) NOT NULL,
  `author` varchar(64) NOT NULL,
  `description` text NOT NULL,
  PRIMARY KEY (`feedback_id`,`language_id`)
);

CREATE TABLE IF NOT EXISTS `oc_feedback_to_layout` (
  `feedback_id` int(11) NOT NULL,
  `store_id` int(11) NOT NULL,
  `layout_id` int(11) NOT NULL,
  PRIMARY KEY (`feedback_id`,`store_id`)
);

CREATE TABLE IF NOT EXISTS `oc_feedback_to_store` (
  `feedback_id` int(11) NOT NULL,
  `store_id` int(11) NOT NULL,
  PRIMARY KEY (`feedback_id`,`store_id`)
);
```

You can run the queries directly in the database, but the easiest way is to copy and save them in a file, such as `feedback.sql`, and import it from the **Administrator** section. Go to **Administrator** | **Tools** | **Backup/Restore**, choose `feedback.sql`, and click on the restore button, as shown in the following screenshot:

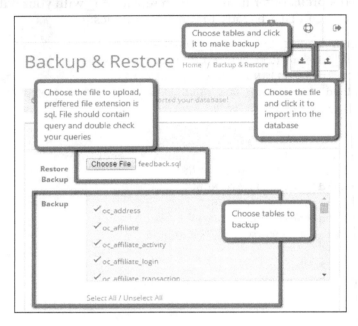

After running the preceding queries, let's begin by creating custom pages in the admin section and executing the **CRUD** (**Create, Read, Update, and Delete**) functionality. To create and update operations, we have to create a form for feedback, and then read the list of feedback with pagination. After this, we will make the frontend pages list the feedback with pagination. As you already know that OpenCart is an MVCL framework, the files that we create need to follow the MVCL pattern. We need to create the files for the feedback as per this screenshot:

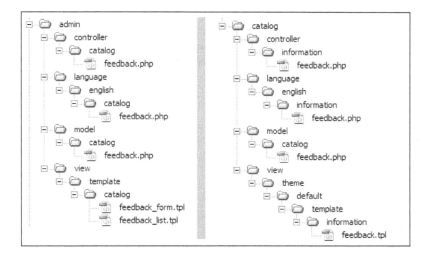

Creating files in the admin section for feedback

In the admin section, we execute the CRUD functionality. For this, we have to create files where we can list all of our feedback and the form to insert or update the feedback, and save them in the respective table of the database. Let's start with the language file.

Creating the language file in the admin section

Create a file in `admin/language/english/catalog/feedback.php`. Then paste the following lines of code in it:

```php
<?php
// Heading
$_['heading_title']          = 'Feedback';
// Text
$_['text_success']           = 'Success: You have modified Feedback!';
$_['text_list']              = 'Feedback List';
$_['text_add']               = 'Add Feedback';
$_['text_edit']              = 'Edit Feedback';
$_['text_default']           = 'Default';
// Column
$_['column_feedback']        = 'Feedback';
$_['column_author']        = 'Author';
$_['column_action']          = 'Action';
```

```
// Entry
$_['entry_author']          = 'Author Name:';
$_['entry_description']      = 'Description';
$_['entry_store']           = 'Stores';
$_['entry_status']          = 'Status';
$_['entry_layout']          = 'Layout Override';
// Error
$_['error_warning']= 'Warning: Please check the form carefully for
errors!';
$_['error_permission']= 'Warning: You do not have permission to modify
Feedback!';
$_['error_author']          = 'Author name must be between 3 and 64
characters!';
$_['error_description']= 'Description must be more than 3
characters!';
$_['error_store']= 'Warning: This Feedback page cannot be deleted as
its currently used by %s stores!';
?>
```

These lines of code are written to describe the text and set the variables that will be accessed in the controller files. You can access the language file in the controller using `$this->load->language('catalog/feedback');`, and its variables using `$this->language->get('name_of_variable');` statements.

Creating the model file in the admin section

To create a model file, you need to go to the `model` folder and then to the required folder. It will be named in the controller like this:

```
$this->load->model('FOLDER_NAME/FILE_NAME_WITHOUT_EXTENSION');
```

Now we can create a file named `feedback.php` in `admin/model/catalog` for feedback. Then we can load the model in the controller using:

```
this->load->model('catalog/feedback');
```

Now it's time to find a unique class name starting with the word `Model`, followed by the folder name, and then the filename without extension. As we are creating the `feedback.php` file in the `admin/model/catalog` folder, the class name for the model will be `ModelCatalogFeedback`, which will extend the parent `Model` class:

```php
<?php
class ModelCatalogFeedback extends Model {
public function addFeedback($data) {
$this->event->trigger('pre.admin.feedback.add',$data);
```

```
$this->db->query("INSERT INTO " . DB_PREFIX . "feedback SET status =
'" . (int) $data['status'] . "'");
    $feedback_id = $this->db->getLastId();
foreach ($data['feedback_description'] as $language_id =>$value) {
$this->db->query("INSERT INTO " . DB_PREFIX . "feedback_
description SET feedback_id = '" . (int) $feedback_id . "',
language_id = '" . (int) $language_id . "', author = '" . $this-
>db->escape($value['author']) . "', description = '" . $this->db-
>escape($value['description']) . "'");
}
if (isset($data['feedback_store'])) {
    foreach ($data['feedback_store'] as $store_id) {
$this->db->query("INSERT INTO " . DB_PREFIX . "feedback_to_store SET
feedback_id = '" . (int) $feedback_id . "', store_id = '" . (int)
$store_id . "'");
    }
}
if (isset($data['feedback_layout'])) {
    foreach ($data['feedback_layout'] as $store_id => $layout_id) {
$this->db->query("INSERT INTO " . DB_PREFIX . "feedback_to_layout SET
feedback_id = '" . (int) $feedback_id . "', store_id = '" . (int)
$store_id . "', layout_id = '" . (int) $layout_id . "'");
    }
}

    $this->event->trigger('post.admin.feedback.add',$feedback_id);
    return $feedback_id;
}
```

These pieces of code show you how to query the database. We need to start with
$this->db->query(), and within the parentheses, we write the SQL query that
we have already covered in the global methods in *Chapter 5, Extensions Code*. In
accordance with the preceding code, we save the feedback, sort order, and status in
the feedback table. Then we retrieve the latest inserted feedback and assigned to the
$feedback_id variable, and the description is looped; you will get the description
as an array because it can consist of multiple languages. It is saved in the feedback_
description table with the feedback ID, language ID, feedback description, and
author of the feedback. As OpenCart supports multistore and multiple layouts, we
must account them. Therefore, after the insertion of the description, we have run the
store query to insert the store, then the layout insertion:

```
public function editFeedback($feedback_id,$data) {
$this->event->trigger('pre.admin.feedback.edit', $data);
$this->db->query("UPDATE " . DB_PREFIX . "feedback SET status = '" .
(int) $data['status'] . "' WHERE feedback_id = '" . (int) $feedback_id
. "'");
```

```
$this->db->query("DELETE FROM " . DB_PREFIX . "feedback_description
WHERE feedback_id = '" . (int) $feedback_id . "'");
foreach ($data['feedback_description'] as $language_id =>$value) {
$this->db->query("INSERT INTO " . DB_PREFIX . "feedback_
description SET feedback_id = '" . (int) $feedback_id . "',
language_id = '" . (int) $language_id . "', author = '" . $this-
>db->escape($value['author']) . "', description = '" . $this->db-
>escape($value['description']) . "'");
}
$this->db->query("DELETE FROM " . DB_PREFIX . "feedback_to_store WHERE
feedback_id = '" . (int) $feedback_id . "'");
if (isset($data['feedback_store'])) {
        foreach ($data['feedback_store'] as $store_id) {
$this->db->query("INSERT INTO " . DB_PREFIX . "feedback_to_store SET
feedback_id = '" . (int) $feedback_id . "', store_id = '" . (int)
$store_id . "'");
        }
    }
$this->db->query("DELETE FROM " . DB_PREFIX . "feedback_to_layout
WHERE feedback_id = '" . (int) $feedback_id . "'");
if (isset($data['feedback_layout'])) {
foreach ($data['feedback_layout'] as $store_id => $layout_id) {
$this->db->query("INSERT INTO " . DB_PREFIX . "feedback_to_layout SET
feedback_id = '" . (int) $feedback_id . "', store_id = '" . (int)
$store_id . "', layout_id = '" . (int) $layout_id . "'");
    }
}

    $this->event->trigger('post.admin.feedback.edit', $feedback_id);
}
```

The preceding queries update the database tables, a row of the feedback table, a row or rows (for multiple languages, if any) of the feedback_description table, a row or rows (for multiple stores, if any) of the feedback_to_store table, and a row or rows (for multiple layouts, if any) of the feedback_to_layout table. First of all, the feedback table's row is updated, but for other tables—feedback_description, feedback_to_store, and feedback_to_layout—all the related feedbacks are deleted first. Then, as per the feedback ID, feedbacks are inserted again. When the feedback table is updated, it deletes all of the related feedback descriptions from the feedback_description table and then inserts the updated data; although no changes are made, it takes them as the new values and inserts them in a loop. The same is done for the feedback_to_layout and feedback_to_store tables:

```
public function deleteFeedback($feedback_id) {
$this->event->trigger('pre.admin.feedback.delete',$feedback_id);
```

```
$this->db->query("DELETE FROM " . DB_PREFIX . "feedback WHERE
feedback_id = '" . (int) $feedback_id . "'");
$this->db->query("DELETE FROM " . DB_PREFIX . "feedback_description
WHERE feedback_id = '" . (int) $feedback_id . "'");
$this->db->query("DELETE FROM " . DB_PREFIX . "feedback_to_store WHERE
feedback_id = '" . (int) $feedback_id . "'");
$this->db->query("DELETE FROM " . DB_PREFIX . "feedback_to_layout
WHERE feedback_id = '" . (int) $feedback_id . "'");
$this->event->trigger('post.admin.feedback.delete',$feedback_id);
}
```

The preceding code is used for deleting the feedback. We have to delete it from all of the tables whenever we run the delete operation. Taking all the feedback tables into consideration, we have to delete from the feedback, feedback_description, feedback_to_store, and feedback_to_layout tables:

```
public function getfeedback($feedback_id) {
$query = $this->db->query("SELECT * FROM " . DB_PREFIX . "feedback
WHERE feedback_id = '" . (int) $feedback_id . "'");
return $query->row;
}
```

This snippet of code is used to retrieve a row. To run a select query, you have to run the query with $this->db->query(). Then assign it to a variable and write it as $Variable_Name->row;. To retrieve a single column and multiple rows, we have to write $Variable_Name->rows;, which returns an array. We need only one row for the specified feedback ID, so we execute the $query->row; command:

```
public function getFeedbacks($data = array()) {
if ($data) {
$sql = "SELECT * FROM " . DB_PREFIX . "feedback f LEFT JOIN " . DB_
PREFIX . "feedback_description fd ON (f.feedback_id = fd.feedback_id)
WHERE fd.language_id = '" . (int) $this->config->get('config_language_
id') . "' LIMIT " . (int) $data['start'] . "," . (int) $data['limit'];
    $query = $this->db->query($sql);
    return $query->rows;
  } else {
$query = $this->db->query("SELECT * FROM " . DB_PREFIX . "feedback f
LEFT JOIN " . DB_PREFIX . "feedback_description id ON (f.feedback_id
= fd.feedback_id) WHERE fd.language_id = '" . (int) $this->config-
>get('config_language_id') . "' ORDER BY f.date_added DESC");
    $feedback_data= $query->rows;
    return $feedback_data;
  }
}
```

All of the feedback from the database is retrieved using the preceding code. If $data is passed, which means that if there are sort order styles, or a limit on the rows to be retrieved, then you need to filter the data from the SQL query and retrieve the required rows. It will retrieve data from the feedback and feedback_description tables, and return it as an array. If it is sorted by the passed data value as per the name or passed data value else by default. If it is sorted by feedback ID, then the limitations on retrieving the rows are applied. The queries are run and the rows are retrieved.

The following code retrieves the description, of the respective feedback_id passed. It will return the description, in all of the languages, in an array:

```
public function getFeedbackDescriptions($feedback_id) {
$feedback_description_data= array();
$query= $this->db->query("SELECT * FROM " . DB_PREFIX . "feedback_
description WHERE feedback_id = '" . (int) $feedback_id . "'");
foreach ($query->rows as $result) {
    $feedback_description_data[$result['language_id']]= array(
            'author' => $result['author'],
            'description' => $result['description']
        );
    }
    return $feedback_description_data;
}
```

The following code, with the method name getFeedbackStores, returns all of the stores to which the specified feedback_id passed:

```
public function getFeedbackStores($feedback_id) {
  $feedback_store_data = array();
$query = $this->db->query("SELECT * FROM " . DB_PREFIX . "feedback_to_
store WHERE feedback_id = '" . (int)$feedback_id . "'");

  foreach ($query->rows as $result) {
    $feedback_store_data[] = $result['store_id'];
  }
  return $feedback_store_data;
}
```

The following code with method name getFeedbackLayouts, will return all of the layouts of the specified feedback_id is passed:

```
public function getfeedbackLayouts($feedback_id) {
$feedback_layout_data = array();
```

```
$query = $this->db->query("SELECT * FROM " . DB_PREFIX . "feedback_to_
layout WHERE feedback_id = '" . (int)$feedback_id . "'");
foreach ($query->rows as $result) {
$feedback_layout_data[$result['store_id']] = $result['layout_id'];
}
return $feedback_layout_data;
}
```

The following code returns the total number of feedbacks:

```
public function getTotalfeedbacks() {
$query = $this->db->query("SELECT COUNT(*) AS total FROM " . DB_PREFIX
. "feedback");
   return $query->row['total'];
}
```

The getTotalfeedbacksByLayoutId() method will return the total number of feedback counts for the specified layout_id passed, and it closes the main model class:

```
public function getTotalfeedbacksByLayoutId($layout_id) {
$query = $this->db->query("SELECT COUNT(*) AS total FROM " . DB_PREFIX
. "feedback_to_layout WHERE layout_id = '" . (int)$layout_id . "'");
   return $query->row['total'];
}


}
?>
```

In this way we have created a model file and run CRUD functionality such as data retrieval, update, insertion, deletion queries. These functionalities will be used on the controller files by loading the model file.

Creating the controller file in the admin section

Now you will look at the controller file of the admin section that controls the code for the insert, list, delete, and form sections. You will get descriptions of each of them. Create a file in admin/controller/catalog/feedback.php. Then go to **Administrator | System | Users | User Groups**. After that, edit the user; in our case, let's edit Administrator. You will see a list of access permissions and modify permissions. Check the box for catalog/feedback for **Access Permission** and **Modify Permission**. With this, you've granted permission for the catalog/feedback link to the Administrator user.

Add a link in the left menu for the feedback management page:

1. Go to `admin/view/template/common/menu.tpl` and find this line of code:

```
<li><a href="<?php echo $information; ?>"><?php echo $text_
information; ?></a></li>
```

2. Below it, add the following line of code. The following code is used to insert the link into the left menu:

```
<li><a href="<?php echo $feedback_link; ?>"><?php echo $text_
feedback; ?></a></li>
```

3. Then go to `admin/controller/common/menu.php` and find this line of code:

```
$data['text_information'] = $this->language->get('text_
information');
```

4. Below it, add the following line of code. This code is used to pass the language variable to the view section:

```
$data['text_feedback'] = $this->language->get('text_feedback');
```

5. In the same file, find these lines of code:

```
$data['information'] = $this->url->link('catalog/information',
'token=' . $this->session->data['token'], 'SSL');
```

6. Below it, add the following code, which creates the link for the controller `catalog/feedback`:

```
$data['feedback_link'] = $this->url->link('catalog/feedback',
'token=' . $this->session->data['token'], 'SSL');
```

7. Go to `admin/language/english/common/menu.php` and insert this at the end:

```
$_['text_feedback']                = 'Feedback Management';
```

Now you are able to access the feedback section through the link. In this way, you can add the link in the left menu. Although it is not recommended to modify the default file, we use it for our convenience and to determine how to find out whether we have to make changes to the default settings. To modify the default files, you are advised to use **vQmod** or **OCMOD**. vQmod is for older versions of OpenCart—before 2.0.2.0. From 2.0.2.0 onwards, OpenCart uses OCMOD, which is similar to vQmod, and this is the way by which we should change the OpenCart default files. You can get more details at `https://github.com/vqmod`.

Now add the following lines of codes to `admin/controller/catalog/feedback.php`:

```php
<?php
class ControllerCatalogFeedback extends Controller {
private $error = array();
```

```
public function index() {
$this->load->language('catalog/feedback');
$this->document->setTitle($this->language->get('heading_title'));
$this->load->model('catalog/feedback');
$this->getList();
}
```

We have created a controller named `ControllerCatalogFeedback`. It is extended from the parent controller. Next, we create an index method that gets loaded by default. Within that, it loads the language files that you have already created, and the title is set with the feedback heading and the `feedback.php` model file:

```
public function add() {
$this->load->language('catalog/feedback');
$this->document->setTitle($this->language->get('heading_title'));
$this->load->model('catalog/feedback');
if (($this->request->server['REQUEST_METHOD'] == 'POST') && $this-
>validateForm()) {
$this->model_catalog_feedback->addFeedback($this->request->post);
$this->session->data['success'] = $this->language->get('text_
success');
$url = '';
if (isset($this->request->get['page'])) {
$url .= '&page=' . $this->request->get['page'];
}
$this->response->redirect($this->url->link('catalog/feedback',
'token=' . $this->session->data['token'] . $url, 'SSL'));
}
$this->getForm();
}
```

When you click on the save button of the form, this method is called. It loads the feedback language file and sets the title of the document to `Feedback` because the `heading_feedback` holds the `Feedback` text. Then it loads the `feedback.php` model file and checks whether the form was submitted or not. If the form was not submitted, then it loads the `getForm()` method from the same `feedback.php` controller file that shows the form. If the form was submitted and validated, then it saves the data in the database, as the `addFeedback` method is called from the model file `$this->model_catalog_feedback->addFeedback($this->request->post);`. The session is set to `success` and redirected to the list of feedbacks:

```
public function edit() {
  $this->load->language('catalog/feedback');
  $this->document->setTitle($this->language->get('heading_title'));
  $this->load->model('catalog/feedback');
```

```
    if (($this->request->server['REQUEST_METHOD'] == 'POST') && $this-
>validateForm()) {
        $this->model_catalog_feedback->editfeedback($this->request-
>get['feedback_id'], $this->request->post);
        $this->session->data['success'] = $this->language->get('text_
success');
        $url = '';
        if (isset($this->request->get['page'])) {
        $url .= '&page=' . $this->request->get['page'];
        }
        $this->response->redirect($this->url->link('catalog/feedback',
'token=' . $this->session->data['token'] . $url, 'SSL'));
    }
    $this->getForm();
}
```

When we click on the edit link, the form page is loaded, as the update method of
this controller is called. It also loads the feedback.php language file, sets the title of
the document, and loads the model feedback.php file. If the submitted data is valid
and the requested method is POST, then it saves the data in the database. Otherwise,
it calls the form again and the form is shown. An update from the controller to the
model is made by the following lines of code:

```
$this->model_catalog_feedback->editfeedback($this->request-
>get['feedback_id'], $this->request->post);
```

This calls the update method of the feedback model. Then the session is set and
redirected to the list of feedbacks:

```
public function delete() {
    $this->load->language('catalog/feedback');
    $this->document->setTitle($this->language->get('heading_title'));
    $this->load->model('catalog/feedback');
    if (isset($this->request->post['selected']) && $this-
>validateDelete()) {
    foreach ($this->request->post['selected'] as $feedback_id) {
    $this->model_catalog_feedback->deleteFeedback($feedback_id);
    }
    $this->session->data['success'] = $this->language->get('text_
success');
    $url = '';
    if (isset($this->request->get['page'])) {
      $url .= '&page=' . $this->request->get['page'];
    }
```

```
    $this->response->redirect($this->url->link('catalog/feedback',
'token=' . $this->session->data['token'] . $url, 'SSL'));
    }
    $this->getList();
}
```

On the feedback list page, when you check the box that is to the left of each row and click on the delete button, the `delete` method of this controller part is executed. It deletes the selected rows from the database and the query that it runs is with the help of `$this->model_catalog_feedback->deleteFeedback($feedback_id);`. It will run in a loop and each selected row will be deleted.

The following is the `getList()` method, which lists all the feedbacks. We are describing only those that are not described earlier. The active page number is set to the `$page` variable and URL is set to the `$url` variable:

```
protected function getList() {
   if (isset($this->request->get['page'])) {
     $page = $this->request->get['page'];
   } else {
     $page = 1;
   }
   $url = '';
   if (isset($this->request->get['page'])) {
     $url .= '&page=' . $this->request->get['page'];
   }
```

In an array, `breadcrumbs` are created and passed to the template file:

```
$data['breadcrumbs'] = array();
$data['breadcrumbs'][] = array(
   'text' => $this->language->get('text_home'),
'href' => $this->url->link('common/dashboard', 'token=' . $this-
>session->data['token'], 'SSL')
);
$data['breadcrumbs'][] = array(
   'text' => $this->language->get('heading_title'),
'href' => $this->url->link('catalog/feedback', 'token=' . $this-
>session->data['token'] . $url, 'SSL')
);
```

Insert and delete links are created and passed to the template file:

```
$data['add'] = $this->url->link('catalog/feedback/add', 'token=' .
$this->session->data['token'] . $url, 'SSL');
$data['delete'] = $this->url->link('catalog/feedback/delete', 'token='
. $this->session->data['token'] . $url, 'SSL');
```

The results ($results) are received by querying the database:

```
$data['feedbacks'] = array();
$filter_data = array(
'start' => ($page - 1) * $this->config->get('config_limit_admin'),
'limit' => $this->config->get('config_limit_admin')
);
$feedback_total = $this->model_catalog_feedback->getTotalfeedbacks();
$results = $this->model_catalog_feedback->getfeedbacks($filter_data);
```

The results received are passed into an array and then to the template file:

```
foreach ($results as $result) {
  $data['feedbacks'][] = array(
    'feedback_id' => $result['feedback_id'],
    'author'      => $result['author'],
    'description' => html_entity_decode($result['description'], ENT_
QUOTES, 'UTF-8'),
'edit'        => $this->url->link('catalog/feedback/edit', 'token=' .
$this->session->data['token'] . '&feedback_id=' . $result['feedback_
id'] . $url, 'SSL')
  );
}
```

Texts are retrieved from the language file and passed to the template file:

```
$data['heading_title'] = $this->language->get('heading_title');
$data['text_list'] = $this->language->get('text_list');
$data['text_no_results'] = $this->language->get('text_no_results');
$data['text_confirm'] = $this->language->get('text_confirm');
$data['column_feedback'] = $this->language->get('column_feedback');
$data['column_author'] = $this->language->get('column_author');
$data['column_action'] = $this->language->get('column_action');
$data['button_add'] = $this->language->get('button_add');
$data['button_edit'] = $this->language->get('button_edit');
$data['button_delete'] = $this->language->get('button_delete');
```

The warning text is set if there is any error warning message returned. Likewise, the success text is set if there is any success message returned:

```
if (isset($this->error['warning'])) {
  $data['error_warning'] = $this->error['warning'];
} else {
  $data['error_warning'] = '';
}
if (isset($this->session->data['success'])) {
```

```
  $data['success'] = $this->session->data['success'];
  unset($this->session->data['success']);
} else {
  $data['success'] = '';
}
```

While deleting feedbacks, `selected` is set in the post method and the `$data['selected']` is assigned those values:

```
if (isset($this->request->post['selected'])) {
  $data['selected'] = (array)$this->request->post['selected'];
} else {
  $data['selected'] = array();
}
```

These pieces of code are used to pass the pagination variable to the template file to show the pagination:

```
$pagination = new Pagination();
$pagination->total = $feedback_total;
$pagination->page = $page;
$pagination->limit = $this->config->get('config_limit_admin');
$pagination->url = $this->url->link('catalog/feedback', 'token=' .
$this->session->data['token'] . $url . '&page={page}', 'SSL');
$data['pagination'] = $pagination->render();
$data['results'] = sprintf($this->language->get('text_pagination'),
($feedback_total) ? (($page - 1) * $this->config->get('config_
limit_admin')) + 1 : 0, ((($page - 1) * $this->config->get('config_
limit_admin')) > ($feedback_total - $this->config->get('config_
limit_admin'))) ? $feedback_total : (((($page - 1) * $this->config-
>get('config_limit_admin')) + $this->config->get('config_limit_
admin')), $feedback_total, ceil($feedback_total / $this->config-
>get('config_limit_admin')));
```

The following code is used to render the `feedback_list.tpl` view on which the header, column, left, and footer are loaded:

```
$data['header'] = $this->load->controller('common/header');
$data['column_left'] = $this->load->controller('common/column_left');
$data['footer'] = $this->load->controller('common/footer');
$this->response->setOutput($this->load->view('catalog/feedback_list.
tpl', $data));
}
```

When we click on the insert button or the edit button, the `getForm()` method is called:

```
protected function getForm() {
$data['heading_title'] = $this->language->get('heading_title');
$data['text_form'] = !isset($this->request->get['feedback_id']) ?
$this->language->get('text_add') : $this->language->get('text_edit');
$data['text_default'] = $this->language->get('text_default');
  $data['text_enabled'] = $this->language->get('text_enabled');
$data['text_disabled'] = $this->language->get('text_disabled');
  $data['entry_author'] = $this->language->get('entry_author');
$data['entry_description'] = $this->language->get('entry_
description');
  $data['entry_store'] = $this->language->get('entry_store');
$data['entry_sort_order'] = $this->language->get('entry_sort_order');
$data['entry_status'] = $this->language->get('entry_status');
  $data['entry_layout'] = $this->language->get('entry_layout');
  $data['button_save'] = $this->language->get('button_save');
$data['button_cancel'] = $this->language->get('button_cancel');
  $data['tab_general'] = $this->language->get('tab_general');
  $data['tab_data'] = $this->language->get('tab_data');
$data['tab_design'] = $this->language->get('tab_design');
```

Texts are retrieved from the language file and passed to the template file. A warning text is set if there is any error warning message returned:

```
if (isset($this->error['warning'])) {
  $data['error_warning'] = $this->error['warning'];
} else {
  $data['error_warning'] = '';
}
```

When `validateForm()` has an error, the error is assigned and shown:

```
if (isset($this->error['author'])) {
  $data['error_author'] = $this->error['author'];
} else {
  $data['error_author'] = array();
}
if (isset($this->error['description'])) {
  $data['error_description'] = $this->error['description'];
} else {
  $data['error_description'] = array();
}
```

The URL is set to the `$url` variable with the page number in the URL:

```
$url = '';
if (isset($this->request->get['page'])) {
  $url .= '&page=' . $this->request->get['page'];
}
```

In an array, `breadcrumbs` are created and passed to the template file:

```
$data['breadcrumbs'] = array();
$data['breadcrumbs'][] = array(
'text' => $this->language->get('text_home'),
'href' => $this->url->link('common/dashboard', 'token=' . $this-
>session->data['token'], 'SSL')
);
$data['breadcrumbs'][] = array(
'text' => $this->language->get('heading_title'),
'href' => $this->url->link('catalog/feedback', 'token=' . $this-
>session->data['token'] . $url, 'SSL')
);
```

This is used to set the action variable for the URL:

```
if (!isset($this->request->get['feedback_id'])) {
  $data['action'] = $this->url->link('catalog/feedback/add', 'token='
. $this->session->data['token'] . $url, 'SSL');
} else {
  $data['action'] = $this->url->link('catalog/feedback/edit', 'token='
. $this->session->data['token'] . '&feedback_id=' . $this->request-
>get['feedback_id'] . $url, 'SSL');
}
```

The following code is used to set the cancel variable with the URL:

```
$data['cancel'] = $this->url->link('catalog/feedback', 'token=' .
$this->session->data['token'] . $url, 'SSL');
```

The following code is used to get the feedback information when you click on the edit button:

```
if (isset($this->request->get['feedback_id']) && ($this->request-
>server['REQUEST_METHOD'] != 'POST')) {
$feedback_info = $this->model_catalog_feedback->getfeedback($this-
>request->get['feedback_id']);
}
```

The following code is used to load active languages:

```
$data['token'] = $this->session->data['token'];
$this->load->model('localisation/language');
$data['languages'] = $this->model_localisation_language-
>getLanguages();
```

When we submit the form by entering the data and it contains an error, isset($this->request->post['feedback_description']) is set to true and the submitted value is assigned to the feedback_description variable, which is passed to the template file. When we click on the edit button, isset($this->request->get['feedback_id']) is true. Data is retrieved from the database and assigned to the feedback_description table. Otherwise, feedback_description will be empty:

```
if (isset($this->request->post['feedback_description'])) {
  $data['feedback_description'] = $this->request->post['feedback_
description'];
} elseif (isset($this->request->get['feedback_id'])) {
  $data['feedback_description'] = $this->model_catalog_feedback-
>getfeedbackDescriptions($this->request->get['feedback_id']);
} else {
  $data['feedback_description'] = array();
}
```

The following code is used for passing the store to the template as with the feedback_description:

```
$this->load->model('setting/store');
$data['stores'] = $this->model_setting_store->getStores();
if (isset($this->request->post['feedback_store'])) {
  $data['feedback_store'] = $this->request->post['feedback_store'];
} elseif (isset($this->request->get['feedback_id'])) {
  $data['feedback_store'] = $this->model_catalog_feedback-
>getfeedbackStores($this->request->get['feedback_id']);
} else {
  $data['feedback_store'] = array(0);
}
```

The following code is used to set the status variable:

```
if (isset($this->request->post['status'])) {
  $data['status'] = $this->request->post['status'];
} elseif (!empty($feedback_info)) {
  $data['status'] = $feedback_info['status'];
} else {
  $data['status'] = true;
}
```

The following code is used to set the layout variable:

```
if (isset($this->request->post['feedback_layout'])) {
  $data['feedback_layout'] = $this->request->post['feedback_layout'];
} elseif (isset($this->request->get['feedback_id'])) {
  $data['feedback_layout'] = $this->model_catalog_feedback-
>getfeedbackLayouts($this->request->get['feedback_id']);
} else {
  $data['feedback_layout'] = array();
}
```

The following code sets the active layouts:

```
$this->load->model('design/layout');
$data['layouts'] = $this->model_design_layout->getLayouts();
```

The following code is used to render the feedback_form.tpl view on which the header, column left, and footer are loaded:

```
$data['header'] = $this->load->controller('common/header');
$data['column_left'] = $this->load->controller('common/column_left');
$data['footer'] = $this->load->controller('common/footer');
$this->response->setOutput($this->load->view('catalog/feedback_form.
tpl', $data));
}
```

The validateForm() method is used to validate the form and needs to be copied just below the getForm() method. It checks for the user's permission on whether to modify the feedback section or not. If it does not have the permission, then an error is shown:

```
protected function validateForm() {
if (!$this->user->hasPermission('modify', 'catalog/feedback')) {
$this->error['warning'] = $this->language->get('error_permission');
}
foreach ($this->request->post['feedback_description'] as $language_id
=> $value) {
if ((utf8_strlen($value['author']) < 3) || (utf8_
strlen($value['author']) > 64)) {
$this->error['author'][$language_id] = $this->language->get('error_
author');
}
  if ((utf8_strlen($value['description']) < 3)) {
    $this->error['description'][$language_id] = $this->language-
>get('error_description');
```

```
    }
  }
  if ($this->error && !isset($this->error['warning'])) {
    $this->error['warning'] = $this->language->get('error_warning');
  }
  return !$this->error;
  }
```

The `validateDelete()` method is used to validate the deletion. First, it checks whether the user has permission to modify or not. If the user has permission to modify, only then the user is able to delete:

```
protected function validateDelete() {
if (!$this->user->hasPermission('modify', 'catalog/feedback')) {
$this->error['warning'] = $this->language->get('error_permission');
}
return !$this->error;
}
```

Creating the template files for form and list pages in the admin section

Go to `admin/view/template/catalog/` and create the `feedback_list.tpl`. Now open `feedback_list.tpl`. You can also check out the sample code where each line is described. The following code used to show the header and the left column:

```
<?php echo $header; ?><?php echo $column_left; ?>
```

The following code block is used to show the add and delete buttons:

```
<div id="content">
  <div class="page-header">
    <div class="container-fluid">
      <div class="pull-right"><a href="<?php echo $add; ?>" data-
toggle="tooltip" title="<?php echo $button_add; ?>" class="btn btn-
primary"><i class="fa fa-plus"></i></a>
      <button type="button" data-toggle="tooltip" title="<?php echo
$button_delete; ?>" class="btn btn-danger" onclick="confirm('<?php
echo $text_confirm; ?>') ? $('#form-feedback').submit() : false;"><i
class="fa fa-trash-o"></i></button>
      </div>
```

The following code is used to show the main title:

```
<h1><?php echo $heading_title; ?></h1>
```

The next code snippet is used to show `breadcrumbs`:

```
<ul class="breadcrumb">
  <?php foreach ($breadcrumbs as $breadcrumb) { ?>
    <li><a href="<?php echo $breadcrumb['href']; ?>"><?php echo
$breadcrumb['text']; ?></a></li>
  <?php } ?>
</ul>
```

The following code is used to show a warning if an error occurs:

```
      </div>
    </div>
    <div class="container-fluid">
      <?php if ($error_warning) { ?>
      <div class="alert alert-danger"><i class="fa fa-exclamation-
circle"></i> <?php echo $error_warning; ?>
        <button type="button" class="close" data-
dismiss="alert">&times;</button>
      </div>
      <?php } ?>
```

The following code shows the success message:

```
<?php if ($success) { ?>
  <div class="alert alert-success"><i class="fa fa-check-circle"></i>
<?php echo $success; ?>
    <button type="button" class="close" data-dismiss="alert">&times;</
button>
  </div>
<?php } ?>
```

The following code shows the panel heading. In our feedback page, it will be
Feedback List:

```
<div class="panel panel-default">
<div class="panel-heading">
  <h3 class="panel-title"><i class="fa fa-list"></i> <?php echo $text_
list; ?></h3>
</div>
```

The following code shows the table heading:

```
<div class="panel-body">
  <form action="<?php echo $delete; ?>" method="post"
enctype="multipart/form-data" id="form-feedback">
    <div class="table-responsive">
```

```
<table class="table table-bordered table-hover">
  <thead>
  <tr>
    <td style="width: 1px;" class="text-center"><input
type="checkbox" onclick="$('input[name*=\'selected\']').
prop('checked', this.checked);" /></td>
    <td class="text-left"><?php echo $column_feedback; ?></td>
    <td class="text-left"><?php echo $column_author; ?></td>
    <td class="text-right"><?php echo $column_action; ?></td>
  </tr>
  </thead>
```

These codes list all the feedbacks. In the first column, a checkbox is shown; in the second column, the feedback description is shown; in the third column, the feedback giver is shown; and in the last column, the blue (edit) button is shown:

```
<tbody>
  <?php if ($feedbacks) { ?>
  <?php foreach ($feedbacks as $feedback) { ?>
  <tr>
    <td class="text-center"><?php if (in_
array($feedback['feedback_id'], $selected)) { ?>
      <input type="checkbox" name="selected[]" value="<?php echo
$feedback['feedback_id']; ?>" checked="checked" />
      <?php } else { ?>
      <input type="checkbox" name="selected[]" value="<?php echo
$feedback['feedback_id']; ?>" />
      <?php } ?></td>
    <td class="text-left"><?php echo $feedback['description'];
?></td>
    <td class="text-left"><?php echo $feedback['author']; ?></td>
    <td class="text-right"><a href="<?php echo
$feedback['edit']; ?>" data-toggle="tooltip" title="<?php echo
$button_edit; ?>" class="btn btn-primary"><i class="fa fa-pencil"></
i></a></td>
  </tr>
  <?php } ?>
  <?php } else { ?>
  <tr>
    <td class="text-center" colspan="4"><?php echo $text_no_
results; ?></td>
  </tr>
  <?php } ?>
  </tbody>
</table>
```

```
      </div>
    </form>
```

If there is no feedback, then **No results** is shown:

```
        <div class="row">
          <?php if ($feedbacks) { ?>
      <div class="col-sm-6 text-left"><?php echo $pagination; ?></div>
      <div class="col-sm-6 text-right"><?php echo $results; ?></div>
            <?php } ?>
          </div>

      </div>
    </div>
  </div>
</div>
<?php echo $footer; ?>
```

Go to `admin/view/template/catalog/` and create the `feedback_form.tpl`. Now open `feedback_form.tpl`. You can also check out the sample code where each line is described. The following code show the save and cancel buttons:

```
<?php echo $header; ?><?php echo $column_left; ?>
<div id="content">
  <div class="page-header">
    <div class="container-fluid">
      <div class="pull-right">
        <button type="submit" form="form-feedback" data-
toggle="tooltip" title="<?php echo $button_save; ?>" class="btn btn-
primary"><i class="fa fa-save"></i></button>
        <a href="<?php echo $cancel; ?>" data-toggle="tooltip"
title="<?php echo $button_cancel; ?>" class="btn btn-default"><i
class="fa fa-reply"></i></a></div>
```

The following line of code shows the main heading. In our feedback example, it shows **Feedback** near `breadcrumb`:

```
        <h1><?php echo $heading_title; ?></h1>
```

The following code is used to show the breadcrumbs:

```
        <ul class="breadcrumb">
          <?php foreach ($breadcrumbs as $breadcrumb) { ?>
          <li><a href="<?php echo $breadcrumb['href']; ?>"><?php echo
$breadcrumb['text']; ?></a></li>
          <?php } ?>
        </ul>
```

The next code snippet is used to show warnings when an error occurs. In our feedback example, if we fill in the author name and description in less than three words, then it gives an error:

```
    </div>
  </div>
  <div class="container-fluid">
    <?php if ($error_warning) { ?>
    <div class="alert alert-danger"><i class="fa fa-exclamation-
circle"></i> <?php echo $error_warning; ?>
      <button type="button" class="close" data-
dismiss="alert">&times;</button>
    </div>
    <?php } ?>
```

The following code is used to show the panel heading. In our example, it shows the **Add Feedback** text:

```
    <div class="panel panel-default">
      <div class="panel-heading">
        <h3 class="panel-title"><i class="fa fa-pencil"></i> <?php
echo $text_form; ?></h3>
      </div>

      <div class="panel-body">
        <form action="<?php echo $action; ?>" method="post"
enctype="multipart/form-data" id="form-feedback" class="form-
horizontal">
          <ul class="nav nav-tabs">
            <li class="active"><a href="#tab-general" data-
toggle="tab"><?php echo $tab_general; ?></a></li>
            <li><a href="#tab-data" data-toggle="tab"><?php echo $tab_
data; ?></a></li>
            <li><a href="#tab-design" data-toggle="tab"><?php echo
$tab_design; ?></a></li>
          </ul>
```

The code you just saw shows the **Feedback** tab like this:

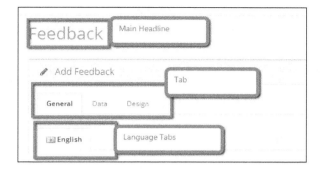

The following code is used to show the **Language** tab:

```
<div class="tab-content">
    <div class="tab-pane active" id="tab-general">
        <ul class="nav nav-tabs" id="language">
        <?php foreach ($languages as $language) { ?>
        <li><a href="#language<?php echo $language['language_
id']; ?>" data-toggle="tab"><img src="view/image/flags/<?php echo
$language['image']; ?>" title="<?php echo $language['name']; ?>" />
<?php echo $language['name']; ?></a></li>
            <?php } ?>
        </ul>
```

The following code you just saw shows the **Author Name** text:

```
<div class="tab-content">
        <?php foreach ($languages as $language) { ?>
        <div class="tab-pane" id="language<?php echo
$language['language_id']; ?>">
            <div class="form-group required">
                <label class="col-sm-2 control-label" for="input-
title<?php echo $language['language_id']; ?>"><?php echo $entry_
author; ?></label>
```

The following code shows the input field to input the author name:

```
<div class="col-sm-10">
    <input type="text" name="feedback_
description[<?php echo $language['language_id']; ?>][author]"
value="<?php echo isset($feedback_description[$language['language_
id']]) ? $feedback_description[$language['language_id']]['author']
: ''; ?>" placeholder="<?php echo $entry_author; ?>" id="input-
author<?php echo $language['language_id']; ?>" class="form-control" />
```

The following code is used to show an error message if someone forgets to enter the author name or the author name is less than three words:

```
<?php if (isset($error_author[$language['language_id']])) { ?>
<div class="text-danger"><?php echo $error_author[$language['language_
id']]; ?></div>
<?php } ?>
```

The following code is used to show the **Description** text:

```
        </div>
    </div>
    <div class="form-group required">
        <label class="col-sm-2 control-label" for="input-
description"><?php echo $entry_description; ?></label>
```

This code shows the text area. Here, the name is given for multiple languages so that it saves on array for multiple data. To show the editor, the `id="description<?php echo $language['language_id']; ?>"` plays a vital role. With the same ID, the following code is called to show the editor:

```
<div class="col-sm-10">
    <textarea name="feedback_description[<?php
echo $language['language_id']; ?>][description]" placeholder="<?php
echo $entry_description; ?>" id="input-description<?php echo
$language['language_id']; ?>" class="form-control"><?php echo
isset($feedback_description[$language['language_id']]) ? $feedback_
description[$language['language_id']]['description'] : ''; ?></
textarea>
```

This is used to show an error message if someone forgets to enter the feedback description or the feedback description is less than three words:

```
<?php if (isset($error_
description[$language['language_id']])) { ?>
        <div class="text-danger"><?php echo $error_
description[$language['language_id']]; ?></div>
        <?php } ?>
```

The following code is written for the **Data** tab:

```php
                </div>
              </div>
            </div>
            <?php } ?>
          </div>
        </div>
        <div class="tab-pane" id="tab-data">
          <div class="form-group">
            <label class="col-sm-2 control-label"><?php echo
$entry_store; ?></label>
            <div class="col-sm-10">
 <div class="well well-sm" style="height: 150px; overflow: auto;">
                <div class="checkbox">
                  <label>
                  <?php if (in_array(0, $feedback_store)) { ?>
<input type="checkbox" name="feedback_store[]" value="0"
checked="checked" />
                    <?php echo $text_default; ?>
                    <?php } else { ?>
     <input type="checkbox" name="feedback_store[]" value="0" />
                    <?php echo $text_default; ?>
                    <?php } ?>
                  </label>
                </div>
                <?php foreach ($stores as $store) { ?>
                <div class="checkbox">
                  <label>
<?php if (in_array($store['store_id'], $feedback_store)) { ?>
<input type="checkbox" name="feedback_store[]" value="<?php echo
$store['store_id']; ?>" checked="checked" />
                <?php echo $store['name']; ?>
<?php } else { ?>
<input type="checkbox" name="feedback_store[]" value="<?php echo
$store['store_id']; ?>" />
                    <?php echo $store['name']; ?>
                    <?php } ?>
                  </label>
                </div>
                <?php } ?>
              </div>
            </div>
          </div>
```

When we click on the **Data** tab, we see stores, as shown in the following screenshot, which are created by the preceding code:

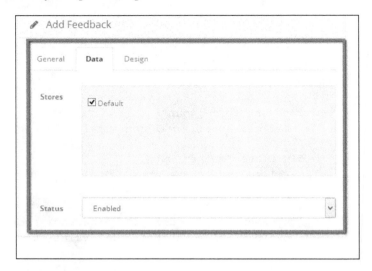

The following code shows the **Status** text and a select box with **Enabled** and **Disabled** options:

```
<div class="form-group">
        <label class="col-sm-2 control-label" for="input-
status"><?php echo $entry_status; ?></label>
        <div class="col-sm-10">
          <select name="status" id="input-status" class="form-
control">
            <?php if ($status) { ?>
            <option value="1" selected="selected"><?php echo
$text_enabled; ?></option>
      <option value="0"><?php echo $text_disabled; ?></option>
            <?php } else { ?>
      <option value="1"><?php echo $text_enabled; ?></option>
            <option value="0" selected="selected"><?php echo
$text_disabled; ?></option>
            <?php } ?>
          </select>
        </div>
      </div>
```

The following code is used to show the default store and the layout select box for the default store under the **Design** tab:

```
          </div>
          <div class="tab-pane" id="tab-design">
            <div class="table-responsive">
              <table class="table table-bordered table-hover">
                <thead>
                  <tr>
        <td class="text-left"><?php echo $entry_store; ?></td>
        <td class="text-left"><?php echo $entry_layout; ?></td>
                  </tr>
                </thead>
                <tbody>
                  <tr>
        <td class="text-left"><?php echo $text_default; ?></td>
<td class="text-left"><select name="feedback_layout[0]" class="form-
control">
                    <option value=""></option>
                    <?php foreach ($layouts as $layout) { ?>
                    <?php if (isset($feedback_layout[0]) &&
$feedback_layout[0] == $layout['layout_id']) { ?>
                    <option value="<?php echo $layout['layout_
id']; ?>" selected="selected"><?php echo $layout['name']; ?></option>
                    <?php } else { ?>
                    <option value="<?php echo $layout['layout_
id']; ?>"><?php echo $layout['name']; ?></option>
                    <?php } ?>
                    <?php } ?>
                  </select></td>
                  </tr>
```

The following code is used to show the stores and its layout in the **Design** tab, just below the default store:

```
                  <?php foreach ($stores as $store) { ?>
                  <tr>
        <td class="text-left"><?php echo $store['name']; ?></td>
<td class="text-left"><select name="feedback_layout[<?php echo
$store['store_id']; ?>]" class="form-control">
                    <option value=""></option>
                    <?php foreach ($layouts as $layout) { ?>
                    <?php if (isset($feedback_
layout[$store['store_id']]) && $feedback_layout[$store['store_id']] ==
$layout['layout_id']) { ?>
```

```
                            <option value="<?php echo $layout['layout_
id']; ?>" selected="selected"><?php echo $layout['name']; ?></option>
                            <?php } else { ?>
                            <option value="<?php echo $layout['layout_
id']; ?>"><?php echo $layout['name']; ?></option>
                            <?php } ?>
                            <?php } ?>
                          </select></td>
                      </tr>
                      <?php } ?>
                    </tbody>
```

With the following JavaScript code, the Summernote editor is activated for the description text-area field:

```
                      </table>
                    </div>
                  </div>
                </div>
              </form>
            </div>
          </div>
        </div>
        <script type="text/javascript"><!--
<?php foreach ($languages as $language) { ?>
$('#input-description<?php echo $language['language_id']; ?>').
summernote({
  height: 300
});
<?php } ?>
//--></script>
```

The following line of JavaScript code is used to activate the first language tab for languages, and to activate the tab functionality:

```
<script type="text/javascript"><!--
$('#language a:first').tab('show');
//--></script></div>
<?php echo $footer; ?>
```

This line is for showing the footer.

Like this, we have completed the changes in the admin section. Now let's move on towards the frontend or catalog folder.

Creating the model file for the catalog folder frontend

We need to create a model file to retrieve data from the database. For this, go to `catalog/model` and create a `feedback` folder. In the `feedback` folder, create `feedback.php` and insert the following code into it:

```php
<?php
class ModelFeedbackFeedback extends Model {
  public function getFeedbacks($data = array()) {
$query= $this->db->query("SELECT * FROM " . DB_PREFIX . "feedback f
LEFT JOIN " . DB_PREFIX . "feedback_description fd ON (f.feedback_id
= fd.feedback_id) LEFT JOIN " . DB_PREFIX . "feedback_to_store f2s
ON (f.feedback_id = f2s.feedback_id) WHERE fd.language_id = '" .
(int)$this->config->get('config_language_id') . "' AND f2s.store_id
= '" . (int)$this->config->get('config_store_id') . "' AND f.status =
'1' ORDER BY f.date_added DESC LIMIT " . (int)$data['start'] . "," .
(int)$data['limit']."");

    return $query->rows;
  }
  public function getFeedbackLayoutId($feedback_id) {
$query = $this->db->query("SELECT * FROM " . DB_PREFIX . "feedback_to_
layout WHERE feedback_id = '" . (int)$feedback_id . "' AND store_id =
'" . (int)$this->config->get('config_store_id') . "'");

    if ($query->num_rows) {
      return $query->row['layout_id'];
    } else {
      return 0;
    }
  }
  public function getTotalFeedbacks($data = array()) {
$query = $this->db->query("SELECT COUNT(DISTINCT f.feedback_id) AS
total FROM " . DB_PREFIX . "feedback f LEFT JOIN " . DB_PREFIX .
"feedback_description fd ON (f.feedback_id = fd.feedback_id) LEFT
JOIN " . DB_PREFIX . "feedback_to_store f2s ON (f.feedback_id =
f2s.feedback_id) WHERE fd.language_id = '" . (int)$this->config-
>get('config_language_id') . "' AND f2s.store_id = '" . (int)$this-
>config->get('config_store_id') . "' AND f.status = '1'");

    return $query->row['total'];
  }
}
?>
```

We created a class named `ModelFeedbackFeedback`, as the `feedback.php` file is created in the `feedback` folder. Then, open it and create a public function called `getFeedbacks`. It queries the database to select all of the data (feedbacks) that has the status `1` from the `feedback` table and the `feedback_description` table. After that, we create a public function called `getFeedbackLayoutId`. It queries the database to get a layout for the feedback. Finally, we create a public function called `getTotalFeedbacks`. It queries the database and counts all the active feedbacks. Then it returns the total number of active feedbacks. The `feedback.php` model file is now ready.

Creating the language file for the frontend

Now go to `catalog/language/english` and create a `feedback` folder. After that, create a file called `feedback.php` and paste the following lines of code into it:

```php
<?php
// Text
$_['text_empty'] = 'There are no feedbacks yet!';
$_['heading_title'] = 'Feedbacks';
?>
```

The required sentences are defined, on the variable and the language file `feedback.php` is created.

Creating the controller file for the frontend

After creating the language and model file, we will create the controller file. Go to `catalog/controller` and create a `feedback` folder. Then create a `feedback.php` file and add the following code into it.

We create a controller class named `ControllerFeedbackFeedback`, as it is in `feedback` folder and the `feedback.php` file. The language file is loaded to get the language using `$this->load->language('feedback/feedback');`:

```php
<?php
class ControllerFeedbackFeedback extends Controller {
  public function index() {
        $this->load->language('feedback/feedback');
```

The following code sets the document title, meta description, and keywords. These are described in the language file:

```php
$this->document->setTitle($this->language->get('heading_title'));
$this->document->setDescription($this->language->get('feedback_
description'));
```

```
$this->document->setKeywords($this->language->get('feedback_
keywords'));
```

The following lines of code are meant for retrieving the message from the language file and passing it to the template file:

```
$data['heading_title'] = $this->language->get('heading_title');
$data['text_empty'] = $this->language->get('text_empty');
$data['button_continue'] = $this->language->get('button_continue');
```

It will set the $page variable to the GET value of the page if GET is set, else $page will be 1. This is needed for pagination. It will set the $limit variable to the GET value of the limit if GET is set, if not $limit will be the value of the catalog limit of the settings from the admin:

```
if (isset($this->request->get['page'])) {
  $page = $this->request->get['page'];
} else {
  $page = 1;
}
```

It adds breadcrumbs which is passed as an array to the template file:

```
$data['breadcrumbs'] = array();
$data['breadcrumbs'][] = array(
  'text' => $this->language->get('text_home'),
  'href' => $this->url->link('common/home')
);
$data['breadcrumbs'][] = array(
        'text' => $this->language->get('heading_title'),
        'href' => $this->url->link('feedback/feedback')
);
```

The $data variable is passed as a parameter to retrieve only a limited amount of the feedback data:

```
$data['feedbacks'] = array();
$limit = $this->config->get('config_product_limit');
$filter_data = array(
        'start'              => ($page - 1) * $limit,
        'limit'              => $limit
    );
```

The `$results` variable retrieves the data, and it is run through the loop to assign only the author name and the feedback description given. Feedback description is stored as encoded HTML, so we have to decode it to show only the formatted HTML. Hence, we parse it with `html_entity_decode`:

```
        $this->load->model('feedback/feedback');
$feedback_total = $this->model_feedback_feedback-
>getTotalFeedbacks($filter_data);
It retrieves the total number of active feedbacks:
$results = $this->model_feedback_feedback->getfeedbacks($filter_data);
        foreach ($results as $result) {
            $data['feedbacks'][] = array(
            'feedback_id'  => $result['feedback_id'],
                'author'        => $result['author'],
'description' => strip_tags(html_entity_decode($result['description'],
ENT_QUOTES, 'UTF-8'))
                );
        }
```

It passes the pagination variable to the template file to show the `$this->data['limit'] = $limit;` pagination:

```
        $url = '';
        if (isset($this->request->get['limit'])) {
            $url .= '&limit=' . $this->request->get['limit'];
        }
$pagination = new Pagination();
        $pagination->total = $feedback_total;
        $pagination->page = $page;
        $pagination->limit = $limit;
$pagination->url = $this->url->link('feedback/feedback', 'path' . $url
. '&page={page}');
            $data['pagination'] = $pagination->render();
$data['results'] = sprintf($this->language->get('text_pagination'),
($feedback_total) ? (($page - 1) * $limit) + 1 : 0, ((($page - 1) *
$limit) > ($feedback_total - $limit)) ? $feedback_total : ((($page
- 1) * $limit) + $limit), $feedback_total, ceil($feedback_total /
$limit));
$data['limit'] = $limit;


$data['continue'] = $this->url->link('common/home');
$data['column_left'] = $this->load->controller('common/column_left');
$data['column_right'] = $this->load->controller('common/column_
right');
```

```
$data['content_top'] = $this->load->controller('common/content_top');
$data['content_bottom'] = $this->load->controller('common/content_
bottom');
$data['footer'] = $this->load->controller('common/footer');
$data['header'] = $this->load->controller('common/header');
```

It checks whether the template file for the current active theme is available or not, and if available, it renders the `feedback.tpl` file. Otherwise, it renders the `feedback.tpl` file from the default theme:

```
if (file_exists(DIR_TEMPLATE . $this->config->get('config_template') .
'/template/feedback/feedback.tpl')) {
$this->response->setOutput($this->load->view($this->config-
>get('config_template') . '/template/feedback/feedback.tpl', $data));
} else {
$this->response->setOutput($this->load->view('default/template/
feedback/feedback.tpl', $data));
}
    }
}
```

Through this, the `feedback.php` controller file is also ready.

Creating the template file for the frontend

Go to `catalog/view/theme/default/template` and create a `feedback` folder. Then create a `feedback.tpl` file and insert this code:

```
<?php echo $header; ?>
<div class="container">
  <ul class="breadcrumb">
    <?php foreach ($breadcrumbs as $breadcrumb) { ?>
    <li><a href="<?php echo $breadcrumb['href']; ?>"><?php echo
$breadcrumb['text']; ?></a></li>
    <?php } ?>
  </ul>
```

The preceding code shows the `breadcrumbs` array.

The following code shows the list of feedback:

```
<div class="row"><?php echo $column_left; ?>
  <?php if ($column_left && $column_right) { ?>
  <?php $class = 'col-sm-6'; ?>
  <?php } elseif ($column_left || $column_right) { ?>
  <?php $class = 'col-sm-9'; ?>
```

```php
<?php } else { ?>
<?php $class = 'col-sm-12'; ?>
<?php } ?>
<div id="content" class="<?php echo $class; ?>">

<?php echo $content_top; ?>
    <h1><?php echo $heading_title; ?></h1>

    <?php foreach ($feedbacks as $feedback) { ?>
     <div class="col-xs-12">
       <div class="row">
            <h4><?php echo $feedback['author']; ?></h4>
            <p><?php echo $feedback['description']; ?></p>
            <hr />
       </div>
     </div>
    <?php } ?>
```

This shows the list of feedback authors and descriptions, as shown in the following screenshot:

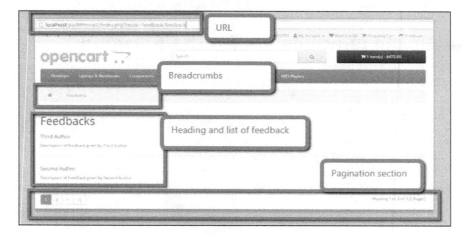

To show the pagination in the template file, we have to insert the following lines of code into whichever part we want to show the pagination in:

```php
    <div class="row">
<div class="col-sm-6 text-left"><?php echo $pagination; ?></div>
<div class="col-sm-6 text-right"><?php echo $results; ?></div>
    </div>
```

It shows the pagination in the template file, and we mostly show the pagination at the bottom, so paste it at the end of the `feedback.tpl` file:

```php
<?php if (!$feedbacks) { ?>
<p><?php echo $text_empty; ?></p>
<div class="buttons">

    <div class="pull-right"><a href="<?php echo $continue; ?>"
class="btn btn-primary"><?php echo $button_continue; ?></a></div>
    </div>
    <?php } ?>
```

If there are no feedbacks, then a message similar to **There are no feedbacks to show** is shown, as per the language file:

```php
    <?php echo $content_bottom; ?>
    </div>
    <?php echo $column_right; ?></div>
</div>
<?php echo $footer; ?>
```

In this way, the template file is completed and so is our feedback management.

You can create a module as described in previous chapters, and show it as a module as well. To view the list of feedback at the frontend, we have to use a link similar to `http://www.example.com/index.php?route=feedback/feedback`, and insert the link somewhere in the templates so that visitors will be able to see the feedback list. Like this, you can extend to show the feedback as a module, and create a form at the frontend from which visitors can submit feedback. You can find these at demo code. Try this first and check out the code if you need any help. We have made the code files as descriptive as possible.

Summary

In this chapter, we created a listing page and a form page, and performed actions such as data retrieval, insertion, deletion, and display it in the frontend. You learned the different ways to manage data. This was achieved by creating pages, listing data, inserting the data into the database, and retrieving data, either to display or to edit. Finally, you saw how to delete the data. Likewise, we showed you how to list the data at the frontend by creating a page. In this way, you will be able to create modules and pages to manage data across OpenCart.

Index

HTML and CSS
  integrating, into OpenCart theme 33
  new theme based on default theme,
    creating 33-35

I

icons, Font Awesome
  about 26, 27
  examples, URL 26
  flipped 28
  rotated 28
image
  height, setting 3-5
  width, setting 3-5
information pages 72

L

language file
  creating, for frontend 178
  creating, in admin section 149, 150
language (language.php) method 124
layouts, module
  configuring 91
Leaner CSS (LESS) 16
length (length.php) method 125
log (log.php) method 125

M

mail (mail.php) method 126
menu style
  changing 51
mixins 21
model file
  catalog/ folder frontend, creating 177, 178
  creating, in admin section 150-155
**Model-View-Controller-Language
    (MVCL) 1**
module
  Banner module, setting 8, 9
  Carousel module, setting 8, 9
  configuring 91
  different layouts, for same module 95
  image dimensions, managing 6
  installing 8, 89, 90
  layouts, configuring 91

layout, managing 9-11
managing, in OpenCart 2.0.1.1 6
position, managing 9-11
positions 93
sort order 94
Slideshow modules, setting 8, 9
status 93
uninstalling 8, 92

O

OCMOD 156
OpenBay Pro 2
OpenCart
  about 1
  features 1, 2
  shop general settings, modifying 2, 3
OpenCart 2
  basic template structure, with
    Bootstrap 17, 18
  Bootstrap, advantages 16, 17
OpenCart 2.0.1.1
  Featured module, configuring 130, 131
  modules, managing 6
OpenCart theme
  about 17, 28
  category page 59
  code, in footer.tpl 51
  code, in header.tpl 35
  contact us page 73
  copyright information, removing
    in footer 55
  CSS of checkout steps, changing 80
  currency style, modifying 46
  files, preparing 31
  footer div style, modifying in footer 54
  header section, checklist 43
  home page 55
  HTML and CSS, integrating 33
  information pages 72
  menu style, modifying 51
  product page 70
  top menu categories code, describing 48
order total modules
  coupon 143
  gift voucher 143
  handling fee 143

Low Order Fee 143
reward points 143
store credit 143
sub-total 143
taxes 143
total 143

P

pagination (pagination.php) method 126
payment module
    about 142
    off-site payment 142
    on-site payment 142
    order total modules 143
product page 70, 71
promotional banner
    creating 7
    setting 7

R

reCAPTCHA
    about 78
    URL 78
request (request.php) method 127
response (response.php) method 127

S

session (session.php) method 128
shipping module
    about 138, 139
    catalog folder, changes 140, 141
    total cost based module, creating 139
shop general settings, OpenCart
    modifying 2, 3
style, for checkout steps
    modifying 80, 81

T

tax (tax.php) method 128
template file
    creating, for frontend 181-183
    for form and list pages, creating 166-176

U

URL (url.php) method 128
user (user.php) method 129

W

weight (weight.php) method 130

Thank you for buying
OpenCart Theme and Module Development

About Packt Publishing

Packt, pronounced 'packed', published its first book, *Mastering phpMyAdmin for Effective MySQL Management*, in April 2004, and subsequently continued to specialize in publishing highly focused books on specific technologies and solutions.

Our books and publications share the experiences of your fellow IT professionals in adapting and customizing today's systems, applications, and frameworks. Our solution-based books give you the knowledge and power to customize the software and technologies you're using to get the job done. Packt books are more specific and less general than the IT books you have seen in the past. Our unique business model allows us to bring you more focused information, giving you more of what you need to know, and less of what you don't.

Packt is a modern yet unique publishing company that focuses on producing quality, cutting-edge books for communities of developers, administrators, and newbies alike. For more information, please visit our website at www.packtpub.com.

About Packt Open Source

In 2010, Packt launched two new brands, Packt Open Source and Packt Enterprise, in order to continue its focus on specialization. This book is part of the Packt Open Source brand, home to books published on software built around open source licenses, and offering information to anybody from advanced developers to budding web designers. The Open Source brand also runs Packt's Open Source Royalty Scheme, by which Packt gives a royalty to each open source project about whose software a book is sold.

Writing for Packt

We welcome all inquiries from people who are interested in authoring. Book proposals should be sent to author@packtpub.com. If your book idea is still at an early stage and you would like to discuss it first before writing a formal book proposal, then please contact us; one of our commissioning editors will get in touch with you.

We're not just looking for published authors; if you have strong technical skills but no writing experience, our experienced editors can help you develop a writing career, or simply get some additional reward for your expertise.

OpenCart 1.4 Template Design Cookbook

ISBN: 978-1-84951-430-9   Paperback: 328 pages

Over 50 incredibly effective and quick recipes for building modern eye-catching OpenCart templates

1. Customize dynamic menus, logos, headers, footers, and every other section using tricks you won't find in the official documentation.

2. A great mix of recipes for beginners, intermediate, and advanced OpenCart template designers.

3. Develop and customize dynamic, powerful OpenCart templates to make your website stand out from the crowd.

OpenCart 1.4: Beginner's Guide

ISBN: 978-1-84951-302-9   Paperback: 240 pages

Build and manage professional online shopping stores easily using OpenCart

1. Develop a professional, easy-to-use, attractive online store and shopping cart solution using OpenCart that meets today's modern e-commerce standards.

2. Easily integrate your online store with one of the more popular payment gateways like PayPal and shipping methods such as UPS and USPS.

3. Provide coupon codes, discounts, and wholesale options for your customers to increase demand on your online store.

Please check **www.PacktPub.com** for information on our titles